Christians
at Work Not Business as Usual

Paul —
Many Blessings !

Jan

Related Books from Herald Press

Jan Wood
Christians at Work

Wally Kroeker, Ben Sprunger, Carol J. Suter
Faith Dilemmas for Marketplace Christians

James Halteman
The Clashing Worlds of Economics and Faith

Calvin Redekop, Benjamin W. Redekop, Editors
*Entrepreneurs in the Faith Community:
Profiles of Mennonites in Business*

John R. Sutherland
Going Broke: Bankruptcy, Business Ethics, and the Bible

John H. Rudy
Moneywise Meditations

Phyllis Pellman Good and Donald B. Kraybill
The Perils of Professionalism

Donald B. Kraybill
The Upside-Down Kingdom

Christians at Work
Not Business as Usual

Jan Wood

in consultation with Beth Oppenlander

A Pandora Press U.S. Book

Herald
Press

Scottdale, Pennsylvania
Waterloo, Ontario

Library of Congress Cataloging-in-Publication Data
Christians at Work : Not Business as Usual / Jan Wood ; in consultation
with Beth Oppenlander.
       p. cm.
    "A Pandora Press U.S. book"
    Includes bibliographical references.
    ISBN 0-8361-9101-3 (alk. paper)
    1. Employees—Religious life. 2. Work—Religious aspects—
Christianity. I. Oppenlander, Beth. II. Title
BV4593.W66 1999
248.8'8—dc21   98-50484
                                                               CIP

The paper used in this publication is recycled and meets the minimum
requirements of American National Standard for Information
Sciences—Permanence of Paper for Printed Library Materials, ANSI
Z39.48-1984.

CHRISTIANS AT WORK
Copyright © 1999 by Herald Press, Scottdale, Pa. 15683
          Published simultaneously in Canada by Herald Press,
          Waterloo, Ont. N2L 6H7. All rights reserved
Library of Congress Catalog Number: 98-50484
International Standard Book Number: 0-8361-9101-3
Printed in the United States of America
Book design by Merrill R. Miller, Herald Press, in collaboration with
Michael A. King, Pandora Press U.S.
Cover design by Merrill R. Miller, Herald Press

08 07 06 05 04 03 02 01 00 99 10 9 8 7 6 5 4 3 2 1

To Patricia,
who made this work possible.

Contents

Preface

What happens at work forms the central content of our lives. It fills our minds both on the clock and off. It structures our time. It shapes our health. It bends our dispositions. It flows into the quality of our relationships—whether for good or ill.

Most of us are bound to work by the necessities of life. Most of us experience tension between our role as worker and our roles as spouse, parent, friend, member of the community, and participant in the community of faith. Yet we who are Christians know our faith extends into and is often deeply expressed through our life of work.

If God is with us, then our work, our workplace, our product become ministry. They are life-giving, filled with adventure and wonder. Infused with new meaning, the entire process of work becomes part of the redemption of a broken world. Our work becomes a sacrament—a visible presence of the invisible works of God.

If through ignorance we fail to see our workplace as the laboratory of the Spirit, we miss our most important mission. We lose an amazing opportunity to join our Master's heart. We stand in danger of being mauled by life-denying world systems. Poor management, downsizing, re-engineering, outsourcing, global economy, and "laws" of economics toss us like rag dolls. We find ourselves in the service of Mammon—even though we really never chose it.

Christians in the Workplace is written to help us all transform the workplace with the love of God. Each of us can enter our own arena of service and make a difference for the kingdom. Each of us has a ministry of Life right where we are. God wants to go to work with us! Empowerment and adventure await us.

> *—Jan Wood*
> *Seattle, Washington*
> *December 1997*

Acknowledgments

Every author's heart is filled with appreciation for persons and occasions that brought the words to the page. I thank Raelene Fendall, Patricia Thomas, Linda Brindle, Bernice Bell, and Becky Wood for prophetic encouragement. They had a vision for my writing before I did. Beth Oppenlander joined with me in collaboration from start to finish. I am grateful for both the joy and productivity of our work together.

Given that time to write came as I recuperated from surgery, I thank the host of friends at Wilmington College and Wilmington Yearly Meeting of Friends who generously gave financial support during those months to liberate me for the writing. I am grateful to Lisa Surdyk, who supplied me with conversation and case studies as background. Finally I thank Belinda Wood, who simply lives out the Good News—and inspires us all.

Part One

POSSIBILITIES

1

God Comes to Work

Those few minutes changed my life. I was standing in a checkout line. The day was hot and humid, the air oppressive to skin and spirit. People milled irritably. Children whined .

I hate standing and waiting. Heat and I are not good friends. Impatience and anger rose in me as my checker seemed to make mistake after mistake. As my turmoil boiled, a thought darted through my mind: *What would this be like if Jesus were standing beside me?* Having no place to go, I thought, *Well, let's pretend Jesus is in line* with me.

To my amazement, something began to happen. It wasn't some idle speculation in my head. I sensed the companionship of a friend. I could imagine the touch of Jesus' hand on my back. And my eyes began to see—*really* see—the people around me.

The mothers looked so weary. Theirs was not the simple tiredness that accompanies a hot, summer day. It was the deep weariness of being poor, of working so hard to make money stretch for family needs. I saw the unhappiness of children whose physical beings but not souls were cared for. I saw something ugly in the human spirit as we all tried to get something for as little as possible. I felt the deep compassion of Jesus for these women and children.

Then my attention was drawn to our checker. Now I saw a woman having a very bad day. She was hot. She was tired. She was in the position of having to fix problems of many other employees who had done their work poorly. I began to look at her with compassion and to simply love her from my heart.

As you might guess, the time flew by. What had seemed interminable waiting now passed in a flash. As I stepped up to the counter, the checker burst into tears and started pouring out the day's woes. My heart turned tender. As she was trying to gain her composure and wipe away the tears so she could see to check my items, she said, "I would have never told you all this, but I could see you really loved me."

I was stricken! I had been among her accusers not ten minutes before. I had blamed her, been angry at her, dumped my irritation on her just like everyone else. I had been adding my piece of pain to this place and these people. If not for the sense of Jesus' presence, I never would have thought to love her. Or had the heart to do so.

This set me to thinking for a long time. It set me to changing my life.

First, it changed how I thought about God's presence. I always knew God was everywhere. God doesn't go away just because I don't think about God. Yet here was a clear example that something new can happen when we make God's presence perceptible. Picturing Jesus was a powerful way to enter the presence of God. Through the ensuing years, I have discovered that there are many ways to make God's presence perceptible in a situation—but Jesus has continued to be one wonderful way I experience God expressing grace.

It was clear to me in this instance and in hundreds that followed that real power is unleashed when God's Spirit is liberated among us. Things happen. People change. Events turn. God's presence is not some internal fantasy that makes my day more pleasant. It is the power that transforms the world.

Second, I became more deeply aware that God's presence meets my needs. In God's Spirit, I am safe. I am loved. I am comforted. I am strengthened. That day in the discount store Jesus' hand was on my back. I could move out of my self-absorption because I was not alone and inward-focused.

Third, I realized the obvious—God sees things from a different perspective! How many times have I not *seen* the other person? The driver on the freeway? My spouse and children? Sales clerks? Bosses? Politicians? Street people? Friends, strangers, beloveds? From whom would I want to withhold the love of God? If I could bring God's presence, power, and love into every situation, what place would I choose to omit?

It was clear that day that God loved each person with the same love extended me. God loves *everyone* with the same attentiveness I've known and treasured. God wants us to see things from divine perspective. God wants us to care about people as God does. God wants us to join the wonder of reaching into a broken world. God has been waiting a long time for us to inquire about God's passions and desires, hopes and dreams, joys and sorrows.

Fourth, it was becoming clear that God's power is realized in those situations in which we join God's viewpoint and heart.[1] I was aware that I prayed constantly about everything for years and years. It wasn't my lack of connection that made a difference—but learning to see from God's perspective!

It's tantalizing to realize that just caring like God does starts a chain reaction that touches others and changes events. The kingdom comes and God's will is done on earth as it naturally is in heaven. And all of us—from least to greatest—have that power when we join God's eyes and heart.

God at Work

The starting place for understanding ourselves as God's people in the workplace is to cultivate the active sense that God doesn't stay at home while we go out to earn the bacon. God wants to be known as a partner in our labor. God wants to extend redemption into the economic realities of our lives. God wants to be present in our work.

So we need to start with some pretty basic questions to ourselves. Where is God while I work? For many, God *is* a

17

constant companion who is at one's side in the workplace. But for others, the thought may seem clumsy. For some, God simply oversees the big plan of our lives while we do the rest with our own wisdom and talents. For others, God cares only if we morally stay within the lines; otherwise, our work is our own business. For some, God is a spiritual thing that stays at church or in the Bible to be taken out for devotions and worship.

If the life and teachings of Jesus are any indication, the Godhead understands work. Tradition has it that Jesus was a skilled craftsman, a carpenter. However, the folks who called him "Rabbi" might not have been giving him an honorary title. He may have indeed gone to rabbinical school and been a rabbi. We know he participated in commercial fishing. He had work-related dinner conversations with tax collectors and women of the night as well as politicians, lawyers, scholars, and teachers. His parables indicate he understood the farmer, the manager, the day laborer, the soldier, the wealthy landowners, the indigent street folk, the rulers and the ruled.

The good news of the gospel is that God has restored us to the family of God. Through Jesus, we all have the privilege of being with God as clearly and wondrously as at the beginning of creation. All that separates us from God's love has been and is being dealt with. We are free to start again. We get to be friends of God. And as friends we gain the privilege of being an extension of God's love and care in the world. We get to participate in the bringing of Heaven to earth here and now. We are part of making all things new and fresh. Bringing God to work is an important part of this adventure.

How Do We Do That?

The first step is to invite God to join us at work. The truth is that God has never been absent from our workplace. But God's Spirit apparently waits to be invited into the various arenas of our lives before the power of God's presence is liberated. God yearns to participate in all aspects of our lives. That's what God created us for. God certainly doesn't need to be begged to do what God yearns to do! But God does await our invitation.

We often need some prompts and reminders to help us stay aware of God-with-us on a normal basis. There are as many different ways to bring ourselves back to the conscious realization of God's Presence as there are types of people. So I am going to suggest a variety of ways people stay mindful of God at work.

• Keeping an ongoing, internal conversation with Jesus through the day.

• Centering ourselves through Scripture, a space of silence, a prayer at regular intervals throughout the work day.

• Thinking a phrase that threads throughout the day like a ribbon. For example—

Be still and know that I am God.
or
Show me how to love today.
or
Thy will be done on earth here as it is in heaven.
or
Jesus is here.

• Placing a reminder in a desk, locker, car, pocket. I have a seashell that reminds me of God's presence. I can keep it in a public place—yet it's a constant prompt of God's loving participation in my life. Just a glance—and I remember. The possibilities vary with the constraints of different work environments. It might be a smooth stone in a pocket. A cross. A watch or a piece of jewelry. A picture. A verse or saying. A plant. Anything will do—even a freckle on your wrist will work if you use it as a trigger to remind you of God's love and attentiveness.

• Using markers of the workday to reawaken consciousness of God's presence. Each job has different markers. Some

19

have coffee breaks. Some have slivers of time between appointments. Some have the movement from one task to another. Find the natural markers of your day and use them to check in with God.

What Can We Expect?

God's presence opens our eyes

The beginning of wisdom is to see. So much of life is lived tragically because we fail to see, *really see*. We can walk by a great idea and miss it because of who said it. We can injure people and never notice the havoc we have caused. We can be so fixated on short-term goals that we squander our future; we trade the infinite for the finite. We make errors in judgment because we didn't see what is at stake. We let ourselves be victims because we can't see the brokenness of the oppressor.

God's presence can open our eyes to the workplace. What does our work look like to God? If we did our job with God's heart, how might we do our work differently? What does God treasure about what we do? How does God see the people we work with, the people we serve, the people affected indirectly by our work? Do our institutional policies implement God's love for everyone? Do I live out consistent love for everyone in the workplace, for persons who receive my product, for those I might affect indirectly?

A friend of mine is a construction contractor. When he began to ask himself these questions, he decided to try an experiment. He knew he was serving people. He knew he was making God's care and provision for the physical needs of people concrete and tangible. He was running his business in an ethical manner. And he was keenly aware of the need to treat his workers fairly and with dignity. But he wondered what would happen if he involved Jesus in the minute-to-minute process of building. He began to look at each piece of lumber, each light fixture, each pipe with new eyes. He imagined that he and Jesus were looking at things together.

To his delight and surprise he began to see things that he had never noticed. He found he noticed defects in the supplies that he normally would have missed. He found himself seeing solutions to problems that had formerly been time-consuming nuisances. He discovered that working with Jesus was wonderful companionship; Jesus *is* good company. And he found that he was saving time, money, and frustration for himself and his customers by eliminating the errors of not really seeing. Seeing is the beginning of effectiveness.

Sometimes we notice selectively. I'm reminded of the religious faculty member polite to colleagues and superiors. A nicer person in the workplace you would never find. Yet this same person treats support staff with astounding cruelty. How could both behaviors come from the same heart? It is a problem of seeing. This professor has never seen the support staff as a person, as an interdependent colleague in the educational task. Has the instructor ever wondered what her secretary's day is like? What it would be like if by a twist of life they were in each other's positions? Or what it might feel like to be carrying out her instructions and responding to her demands? Seeing is the beginning of compassion, mercy, and justice.

The workplace will never be utopia. Any workplace is a collection of broken people with issues and problems of their own. Most jobs ask that we lay aside much of our personal baggage when we come to work. Yet of course we can't totally do that. We *are* affected by the fight we had with our teenager. We do bring our fears about paying the bills to the table when we make decisions. We do have personality quirks and foibles that color the way we do our tasks. We do carry the pain of a parent into the relationship with the boss. We do cope at work in similar ways to the way we cope with the rest of our lives. These are real people with complex lives who are struggling to accomplish the tasks. Folks will never function like stainless steel robots. Seeing is the beginning of understanding. Understanding is the door to effective problem solving.

Everyone's work holds different things to be seen. We all have different kinds of responsibilities for what we see. Yet everyone can have fresh eyes to see the workplace. Only when we truly see can we be parts of the world's solutions rather than adding to the world's problems.

God's presence changes us

God is with us. And if God is with us, then we are safe. We are loved—even cherished. It is part of human nature to be one's best self when we feel safe, secure, treasured. We become more fair-minded, more generous, more able to think wisely and inclusively. Our competencies increase. Being consciously aware of God-with-us makes a profound difference in our own ability to work well. It liberates us from the tyranny of self-absorption that poisons us and everyone around us. It energizes us as we no longer expend so much effort being self-protective. It releases creativity and joy that had been closed to us. In God's presence, we become the people we had always hoped to be.

God's presence changes others

Conversely, freedom and joy in God's Spirit have a domino effect on people we encounter. These qualities invisibly invite others to drop their swords and shields. Folks often sense the new air of safety and care that makes it possible simply to relax and be their best selves. This dramatically changes the human dynamic! It changes workplaces. It changes families. It changes societies and nations.

God's presence changes our available resources

The world's natural systems are bounded and closed. Time is finite; resources are limited; potentialities are often dualistic. We become pinched, circumscribed, self-protective. Either—or. You or me. Win or lose. Have or have not. Live or die.

God Comes to Work

The realm of God breaks into the finite. That is a consistent message of Scripture and experience. Potentialities become limitless. God creates, expands, restores.[2] Our physical and material world is *not necessarily* closed and bounded when we operate in God's presence. We see examples of oil and grain never running out during a famine[3] or the jar of oil that miraculously stretches to fill a village of containers and thus provides more than enough income.[4] We remember the sandals of the wandering Hebrews that never wore out.[5] Or the few loaves and fish multiplied to feed multitudes.[6] In contemporary times we know of Corrie ten Boom's little medicine bottle that didn't run dry during her imprisonment.[7] Or the times our own gas tanks have fed the engine until we reach a safe destination. Or our incomes that somehow stretch to meet our needs.

The tyranny of time is broken. The miracle of the Sabbath rest is re-enacted every week. What would normally consume seven days is finished in six. The promise of the sabbatical year is that miraculous provision will always be made to cover the year of rest.[8] The sun stood still at Ai.[9] Death no longer constricts us with its boundaries.[10]

We experience the marvelous ways too-much-to-do is squeezed into the time available. Inner healing is another way to transcend the limitations of time as we are touched by the presence of God making each moment of the past a moment in the present. In the realm of God, we become participants in the infinite.

When we participate with God in the workplace, we begin to discover that there are worlds of new possibilities open to us! These new possibilities are the trademarks of God's people. They are natural by-products of living life in God's Spirit. They are the sign that God has indeed come to dwell among us. The culture of God is good news in the world of work!

DISCUSSION QUESTIONS

1. Who are the people we don't really *see* during any given day?

2. Who are the people who elicit our compassion? Who are the people who do not?

3. What are the ways I have found useful to remind me of God's presence throughout the day?

4. What is God proud of in our work? What aspects trouble God?

5. What examples have we experienced of God's presence changing a situation? Have we experienced having resources—of time, money, or possibilities—expand?

2

What's God Up To?

Christians are supposed to be standouts. They stand out for wholesomeness, integrity, competence, clear motives, regard for the welfare of others. Christians understand the narrative of Daniel, Meshach, Shadrach, and Abednego.[1] We understand that we live and work in a culture not our own. In that foreign culture, we live out our alignment with God regardless of consequences. The result of such courageous choices is accomplishing amazing things, becoming salt and light to the world. Ordinary people—in the power of God—become the best things that ever happened to this old world. We change things. Light shows the way. Salt preserves things from spoilage and spices things up. God's people are to do the same.

By and large Christians have not begun to tap into the incredible power of God in the world of work. Christians have swallowed the paradigms of the business world hook, line, and sinker. We evidently forgot even to wonder if this is the way Jesus wanted us to live and work. In fact, we have gone the *opposite* direction. We have been making the church a business—and neither the world of business nor of the church is a transforming agent of God in the world.

Back to Our Abc's

To understand our place in the world, we need to review the basics. Our faith begins with the conviction that God created us—and the world around us—for partnership and enjoyment. The first chapter in Genesis is an anthem to the glory of

God's intentions. The Godhead is incredibly generous. Humans are made in the very image of Godness. We are indeed "chips off the ol' block." Work was meant to be a joyous partnering with God. Work, at this point in the human experience, was not drudgery. It was not tied to survival; it was the natural, shared adventure of God and humans.

Well, we all know the narrative. The nature of work changed drastically when humans mistrusted God's good intentions. The narrative of the fall in Genesis 3 is a wise and sophisticated map of the human psyche. The crux of the problem was really not the actual disobedience. The temptation hinged on the argument that God's love and care could not be trusted, that God was not telling the truth. Listen to the words:

> We may eat of the fruit of the trees of the garden; but God said, "You shall not eat of the fruit of the tree which is in the midst of the garden, neither shall you touch it, lest you die."
>
> But the serpent said to the woman, "You will not die. For God knows that when you eat of it your eyes will be opened, and you will be like God, knowing good and evil."

This was the turning point. Once humans decided God's trustworthiness was up for grabs, they turned to their own resources. That's what the story indicates: Humans check it out. Seems a good idea to be wise. Hmmm, yes. It does taste good.

So the shift in our consciousness was made. God's trustworthiness was on trial situation by situation; now the ultimate guides to decision making were human senses and reasoning.

This broke the bonds of trust between humans and creator. The results were immediate and devastating. Guilt. Shame. Vulnerability. Fear and discord with nature. Brokenness of mutuality and equality between men and women. The tyranny of work in pursuit of survival. Death.[2] "Humpty Dumpty had a great fall. All the king's horses and all the king's men could not put Humpty Dumpty together again."

Yet the entire rest of Scripture is the story of God's un-
failing love and faithfulness as we are given opportunity to return to the Garden of unbroken trust with our Creator. George
Fox, the early Quaker, called it "going back through the flaming
sword."[3] The bottom line of our Christian experience is that
Jesus has made it possible for us to rejoin God's heart and intentions in a relationship of trust. As we live into that new ordering of our feelings, choices, and actions, we shed the consequences of alienation.

Now we're no longer driven by guilt and shame. We're
safe to be "just as we are without one plea." We're knit back
into harmonious relations with other humans and nature.
Work again becomes a natural outflowing of our being. And
death no longer blackmails us with threats of annihilation. The
Gospels call the new order the kingdom of God. We live here
and now as we would be living if we were citizens of heaven. If
everyone will love one another when we get to heaven, then we
love like that now. If truth telling will be normal in heaven,
then we make that the norm here as well. If we know God will
take perfect care of us in heaven, then we live on the assumption that God is taking perfectly good care of us now.[4]

In Colossians 1, the Apostle Paul uses the language of im-
migration to explain our situation. When we're knitted back
into God's heart through Jesus, we leave those systems of this
world based on mistrust of God and reliance on human senses
and wisdom. We immigrate to the culture of God, the culture
of the Garden. This culture starts with the *given* that God is
trustworthy, that God has our best interests at heart, that it's
safe again to relax totally into the presence of God.

The culture of God does not expect us to have to go it
alone. The culture of God is not some punitive system in which
the Godhead is sitting critically on the sidelines waiting to
pounce on us for failure. The culture of God calls us to live our
complex lives in the simplicity of partnering with God and
letting the rest of life follow in the wake. "Seek ye first the

kingdom of God and all these things will be added unto you."[5] Or as Jesus phrased it, we are in the world but not of it.[6]

We live, work, experience life in a setting of brokenness and alienation from trusting God. Yet *right amid that world*, we live a totally different system based on radically different premises. The picture here is not of a safe and isolated haven from a broken world. Rather, as John Fischer describes it, Christians are called to "infuse the customs, civilizations, and achievements of every age and society with people who love and fear God."[7] We live amid the fray but by new values, choices, priorities. God goes to work with us—and work becomes different! True, our lives flower and bear a different fruit from the world around us. But it is also true that our presence in the world should change it!

So what are these radically different premises that make all the difference in the world? We explore them next.

God Loves Us and Has our Best Interests at Heart

So pervasive is our mistrust of God that we routinely misread Scripture. Doesn't our usual interpretation of the Genesis narrative go something like this? "Well, God was really angry at Adam and Eve for disobeying. So he kicked them out of the garden to punish them." Look again at Genesis 3:20–4:1.

> The man called his wife's name Eve, because she was the mother of all living. And the Lord God made for Adam and for his wife garments of skins, and clothed them.
>
> Then the Lord God said, "Behold, the man has become like one of us, knowing good and evil; and now lest he put forth his hand and take also of the tree of life, and eat, and live forever"—therefore the Lord God sent him forth from the garden of Eden to till the ground from which he was taken. He drove out the man; and at the east of the garden of Eden he placed the cherubim, and a flaming sword which turned every way, to guard the way to the tree of life.
>
> And now Adam knew Eve his wife, and she conceived and

bore Cain, saying, "I have gotten a man with the help of the Lord."

The ancients traditionally talked of consequences of behavior in terms of blessings and curses. This is the language that frames the Genesis 3 narrative—and sometimes confuses us about the heart of God. Maybe we can understand it better if we think of it in terms of God describing the consequences of the human choice: This is what was at stake. This is what the human situation is going to look like.

Yet God doesn't proceed punitively. The woman is honored as the mother of the human race. God compassionately sacrifices the precious animals of creation to clothe and care for the new physical needs of the human condition. The Godhead turns humans finite—for now living forever will be torture rather than blessing. Can you imagine having to live with the consequences of our woundedness, brokenness, and violence without an end? God would be doing us no favor by trapping us eternally in the consequences of our choices.

I doubt God drove the human race from the proverbial garden in anger. This was an incredible act of mercy. And it is important to notice that eternal life was restored to humans as soon as provision was available for us to be reconciled again with God. We glimpse God's thorough love for humanity in the verses of I Peter that indicate Jesus even preached to those who had previously died, so all humanity could be knitted back into the love of God.[8]

> For God so loved the world that he gave his only Son, that whoever believes in him should not perish but have eternal life. For God sent the Son into the world, not to condemn the world, but that the world might be saved through him.[9]

Well and good. But if God so loves us and so wants good things for us, why is life so hard? Why do people I love die? Why does tragedy strike good people who don't deserve it? Why are children allowed to starve? Why aren't my prayers for good answered? The original sin in all of us loves what theologians call a theodicy. How can a powerful, loving God allow the suffering of the human condition?

Aha. Now we have good cause for not trusting God! Back to square one. Life is hard because we continue to reap the consequences of human choices over centuries. God is leading us back to the Garden. The kingdom is come. But this means we must trust the Creator's love amid a still-broken world.

God Wants Transformation, Not Control

What is the way out? Or perhaps we should say, the way back? We start with the premise of God's trustworthiness. We let God inform our hearts and emotions rather than placing God on trial and demanding an explanation. Then perhaps we begin to appreciate God's choices. God has made one commitment to humans that seems inviolate. God allows us to choose—even if the consequences are dire. The essential ingredient of being human seems to be choice. As long as God honors choice in us, God has self-limited God's power to make everything right. Things become "right" as we align our actions and behaviors with God's hopes, dreams, wisdom.

However, as long as we live in a world where some folks are choosing God and some trusting their own senses and wisdom, we'll experience events that don't go God's way. God has no desire for people to be torn from dear ones through death. God takes no pleasure in our fears and anxieties. God isn't withholding when the miracle doesn't happen.

To make a perfect world for us, God would have to control and manipulate each of us. And God has promised not to do that. But God's not standing idly by. God has made it possible to take the worst life can throw at us and transform it into something useful, life-giving, eternally valuable. Jesus is the best example of God's strategy of transformation!

The worst thing that could have happened in the universe happened. It started well; God made flesh God's love and compassion and joined the human experience in Jesus. Here was God's love walking, talking, eating, playing, working. Doing no harm. Healing. Enlivening. And human choice said, "No thank you! We'd rather do it ourselves, our way." So they killed God and valued a common criminal. It can't get much worse than that.

Yet God used the lowest point of the human experience to become the very salvation of the human race. Love couldn't be put to death. It couldn't stay dead and entombed. It could descend to the pit of human nothingness, but it rose, releasing the spirits of all who want life. The worst became the most precious. The ultimate sin became the greatest gift.

The same miracle happens in and through God's people on a daily basis. The handicapped child is born; we think we've been abandoned by the love of God. But lo and behold! Love, pleasure, and wonder in the child strangely supplant the sadness. The beloved dies, yet new purpose rises amid the loss. The disease robs us of some abilities and gives us the gift of other experiences. Death seems to sever but in fact connects us eternally. Thus the vision of God's people in the culture of God is not to avoid all difficulties in life; rather, it's to accept what life brings and to be a transforming agent in every situation.

Thus sin and evil are vanquished because they cease to have the power to quench the human spirit, to dampen the love of the creator, to squeeze life from the eternal endeavor. And by the genius of God's wisdom, what would naturally have been death-producing becomes useful and precious. Amazing! It becomes totally true that "all things work together for good" to those who participate in the transforming love of God.[10]

God the Creator Knows How the World Works

It would seem to go without saying that God—who has created everything—knows how things work. It's such a simple observation that it feels silly to dwell on it; yet part of our condition of mistrust is that we lose sight of this reality. God knows the laws of the physical universe better than we do. God totally understands things that we haven't even begun to discover yet. Our human knowledge base is only a fraction of the complete wisdom of the Creator.

So if God says the way for the human body and spirit to thrive is to rest and relax in a ratio of one to six, then wouldn't it be wisdom for stressed-out folks to think, "God knows something I don't. I'd better look into this."?[11] If God tells us through Jesus that the only way to achieve long-term success in a conflict is to love the enemy, then shouldn't that be the rule of thumb for God's people?[12] If God has given us a vision of organizing the human endeavor around giftedness and use of people's God-given strengths, why do we still whittle people down to fit jobs rather than allowing jobs to fit people?[13]

So the question becomes painfully obvious. We must be ignoring the wisdom of God because we don't fully grasp that instruction is given for our success, our benefit. For instance, when we buy a new car we're given an instruction book. I for one am grateful for this little volume. I know it will help me keep my car working at its best. I don't see the car manufacturers as putting that book in the glove compartment to lord it over me. I don't question whether they understand the designs they've created. I know they've given these instructions to maximize my success and pleasure with my vehicle.

So it is with God. God doesn't give us instructions to play power games with us. God is letting us in on the mysteries and solutions of the universe! Human brokenness may have obscured the reality. It may be contrary to our senses. But God is constantly giving us the wisdom of the Eternal. And it's free!

Obedience Is Alignment with God's Wisdom

In this light, obedience is not a bending of wills, a childish submission, a giving up of personhood. Obedience to the Holy, Living God is an act of tremendous good sense. Here is a God who knows how things work, who loves us and has our best interests at heart, who is willing to share the secrets of success. Why wouldn't we take the tips and run with them! We gamble on far less substantial information in our life. We turn left on an interstate cloverleaf when we know we need to end up going to our right. Why? Because we trust the designers of the highway.

We submit to surgeries and medical procedures that make us deathly ill in the hopes we will get well. Why? Because we trust the science and the process. We are willing to gamble our savings on a guess about what the economy will do in the stock market. Why? Because we believe there may be a payoff on our risk.

Yet when God's wisdom seems to run counter to our senses, we balk. "I can't reserve a day a week for rest and relationships with God, family, and friends—I have too much to do." And we don't. When God's wisdom indicates that the way to wholeness is through submission to situations we'd rather avoid, we bristle at the thought. Unthinkable. And when God's wisdom leads us to trade the temporal for the eternal, we deem it a risk not worth taking.

Interesting. How do we account for this? Again it must be that we haven't believed God is on our side, that God wants the best for us—and is leading us to it as surely as the sun rises. In a sense we have much in common with our Aztec brothers who thought they had to sacrifice life each morning to accomplish what God was going to do for them anyway.[14]

Obedience is the relaxing, wonderful choice to follow God's lead, to participate in the Divine Wisdom. Obedience is like a dance. Sometimes in the dance the movements are identical. Sometimes the moves mirror one another. Sometimes there is a weaving of comings and goings of many dancers moving to a caller's voice or the choreographer's plan. Sometimes there is simply the sway of affection and care. The discipline of learning the steps and rhythm of the dance is usually considered a joy. Obedience to the dance would rarely be thought punitive or too demanding. The dance liberates our bodies and spirits in amazing ways. It connects our heart to other dances. So does the dance with God.

There Is No Separation Between Sacred and Secular

Everything is part of God's world. God did not create the world, then become constricted to a little corner of existence called "the sacred" or "the spiritual." The Hebrew Scriptures, the Old Testament, reflect this total involvement of God in human affairs. God participated in *all life*. Whether in issues as ordinary as "What's for dinner?" or as weighty as the choice of national government, God was there. Inner thoughts. Sexuality. Hygiene. Work. Welfare. Holidays and play. Worship and ethics. Family life. Government. Art and creativity. There was no corner of life in which God did not participate.

God's wisdom was good for pleasure as well as pain. God's directions created business tycoons like Jacob as well as cared for the disenfranchised and the poverty-stricken like Ruth. These artificial walls we in the West have erected between sacred and secular are bogus. The same love that solves problems in the chapel solves problems in the boardroom, on the factory floor, amid politics. The prayer that saves our sanity in the privacy of our spirit is the same prayer that participates in the healing medical processes. Principles of honesty and integrity that are the basis of a Christian's spirituality are the same ones undergirding a Christian's business practices. God's partnership, God's empowerment, God's miracles, God's grace and forgiveness extend to every corner of our existence. God wishes fully to participate in our vacationing and our service. God's intentions are to be a partner with us in *all* life.

How rude we are to tell the Living God where the Divine Presence is acceptable and where it isn't! How dare we bar the Creator from the Godhead's own creation? What impudence to think we decide where and how God can and can't work! Amazing, isn't it? The truth is that God wants to do business with us. As with Abraham, Jacob, Joseph, and the hosts of God's people who came after them, God loves to help people prosper in their work and endeavors. So whether it is Brother Lawrence washing pots and pans with God in a seventh-century monastery[15] or R. G. Le Tourneau going into conscious partnership with God to make heavy earthmoving equipment,[16] God delights in bringing the fullness of God's presence and capabilities to the workplace.

We're Working on an Eternal Continuum

The choices of a wise investor will be different based on the length of investment. A short-term choice of stock may be far different than one intended to be kept for many years. So it is with our choices in life and work.

One of the wiser pieces of advice I've received came from my father. He was teaching me to drive. I was having trouble keeping the car on a steady course. I jiggled us this way and that as I made constant steering corrections. My father watched me, then said, "Don't look at the hood ornament. Look at the end of the road. The car will follow your eye."

This seemed too good to be true. But sure enough—when I simply looked down the road at the end of the curve, the car traveled smooth and sure. Since that driving lesson, I've learned my father's advice is useful for more than driving. When we're too shortsighted, our life choices become erratic and costly. They jiggle us this way and that. When we keep focused on the horizon, we find our course efficient and effective.

Our life in the workplace is catastrophically damaged because of our aiming for the hood ornament! Scripture, the words of Jesus, the experiences of those who have died and been revived, and the witness of our own spirit—all these sources tell us life is eternal. Our work is one part of our total contribution to the human race, to the universe. Our work is much larger than the paycheck or things it brings us.

Our work is an eternal contribution. Are we not still eating fruit from the trees planted by our ancestors? Are we not still using ideas born of the ancients? Am I not drawing electrical energy for this computer from the hydroelectric power created by the dam my grandfather helped construct? Today each of us is benefiting from the goodness of choices made 1,000 generations ago![17] That's how long each God-aligned choice will bear fruit! The life expectancy of goodness is infinite.

I'm constantly amazed and delighted at how long I draw strength and joy from experiences long past. It was years ago that the person who took my call at the telephone company spoke to me in such kind tones. Yet that kindness remains a tender encouragement in my heart. That woman has no idea how her kindness continues to bear fruit!

Or take the car rental agent who extended herself far beyond normal customer service. Yes, her company will prosper. She will probably receive promotions and advancement. She has also made eternal deposits in my life that will never end.

How many smiles and greetings of strangers have warmed my heart and given me encouragement? How many services have been offered with such generosity of spirit that moves me to gratefulness and appreciation? How many times has power been used to help me be everything I can be? Any labor aligned with God's heart bears eternal fruit.

So deciding between the catty retort to the customer and the compassionate response is choosing for wasting precious energy while pouring toxic waste into your own and other's cells—*or* for offering a moment of care that will pay dividends until the end of time. In that light, the brief pleasure of letting "them have it" is hardly worth it. Thomas Kelly, a twentieth-century philosopher, calls this perspective "living in the Eternal Now."[18] This marvelous phrase helps keep us focused on making short-term choices in light of long-term consequences.

Donald Kraybill in *The Upside-Down Kingdom* says it so well:

The future is already present among these [God's] people. They are citizens of a future kingdom which is already here. These are the people who turn the world upside down because they know there is another King named Jesus. These children of the Most High welcome the reign of God each day with the words, "Thy kingdom come, they will be done on earth as it is in heaven."[19]

Many Christians have the mistaken notion that what we're doing here and now is somehow disconnected from eternal life. But we're part of the eternal right now. What we are, what we're choosing, and how we're investing our time and energy are already weaving the fabric of our infinite existence— for better or for worse. God doesn't need to send us to hell. We choose to create hell now when we choose to live separated from the love and power of God. That choice will be honored after time as we know it has passed. When we choose to snuggle into the heart of God and live out of God's presence, we become part of heaven now. And that which is of God never perishes.[20]

DISCUSSION QUESTIONS

1. In what ways is it easy to know God is trustworthy? When does it feel like God has broken trust?

2. What evidences has God given me personally that God is indeed trustworthy?

3. What are examples of transformation in Scripture? In our church's history? In the life of our congregation? In my life?

4. Does obedience feel like a joyful privilege? Why or why not?

5. What are the areas of my life that I separate from God's presence?

6. What things do we think are going to count in the long run? Are those the things to which I'm giving the most energy and attention now?

Gospel Order in the Workplace

I've been a Christian since I was a small child. I was privileged to absorb the message of the church through my social environment as well as personal discovery. This had its gifts and its weaknesses. One subtle message I took in over the years was something like this: "God wants us to give our lives to him. This will require us to sacrifice everything we want and enjoy, but it will be worth it because we will have eternal life." When I used to read the principles of the kingdom,[1] I thought they were just more of this tough stuff God was asking of me.

It felt like the noose just tightened around my spiritual neck. For instance, now it wasn't enough to maintain moral sexual *action*. Now I had to control my unbidden *thoughts* as well! I tried to be nice to everyone, but now I was supposed to love the enemy! Who did God think I was? Supergirl? I wasn't finding the Gospel Order to be good news at all. In fact, I simply avoided it in favor of other passages of Scripture I liked a lot better.

Then one day God turned my world right side up! I had always noticed that the New Testament speaks of the kingdom of God or kingdom of heaven.[2] Over 100 times the phrase is used. All that time I had assumed this meant that when we got to heaven or when the millennial kingdom came, life would look like these verses. When the kingdom came there would be harmony, joy, freedom, love—all that good stuff.

Gospel Order in the Workplace

My earthshaking realization was that Jesus had brought the kingdom here to earth for all of us to participate in here and now! The same qualities I was so looking forward to in the by and by could be experienced and nurtured *now*. You've got to be kidding! As I wrote that day,

> Jesus came to transform our here and now distress into "mini-millenniums [sic]." The perfect reign of Jesus can be realized in each area of my life as I am obedient to his rule. That means that if I begin to follow the principles of Jesus' kingdom in my relationships at work, then I can expect that Jesus' reign is realized there. I can expect healing, wholeness, miracles and change. I can expect that Jesus' lordship is extended over every area of life in which I am obedient."[3]

Whew! This made it a whole new ball game for me! I so wanted the world to be better. Now I was seeing that I was not a helpless victim waiting it out until Jesus set things right in heaven. Jesus had already made provision for us to join God in setting it right. The kingdom starts now and continues forever. So all this hard stuff I was reading wasn't some higher hurdle to taunt me—but the gate through which the world can and will be changed.

The second realization was cousin to the first. I realized there are two systems in the world. There is the world's system. And there is God's system. God's system is the way things really work. The world's system is a counterfeit. It looks like it will work. It looks easier, faster, more practical. The only problem: the world's system is a lie. It is a bundle of shortcuts that don't finally work. They take everything from us. Money will never bring security. Lust doesn't bring us love. Domination doesn't bring us respect. Yet such strategies entice us because they have come to seem the "real world." They govern how we think, react, exist. They form the basis of business, advertising, entertainment, corporate life and structure, educational systems, governments, moral and ethical milieus. Folks often even think the strategies of the world system should run the church.

We absorb the world system like the air we breathe. But the bitter reality of this counterfeit system is that it cannot bring us what we long and hope for. It doesn't and can't work because it's disconnected from the source of true life. It can't bring permanent peace, joy, love, wholeness, security, success, and life. Its legacy is brokenness, alienation, fear, stress, inadequacy, pain . . . and death.

God's system, on the other hand, actually does bring us the deep desires of our hearts. It's effective because it reflects the very nature of the Creator and is consistent with the way Creation works. It's effective because God knows us. God knows how we "tick." God loves us and knows the ways forward in our lives. The Gospel Order isn't some pie-in-the-sky expectation of a mysterious, aloof, demanding God; it's the gracious instructions manual for success. In fact I was astounded to realize that the kingdom instructions answer questions as contemporary as your latest television commercial:

- how to be successful, great, a leader;
- how to "win" in light of our weaknesses and failures;
- how to overcome and transform angry, hateful, hurtful, people;
- how to deal with tragedy, sorrow, and loss;
- how to transform every aspect of our worlds;
- how the church can be a place of power, the face of God for the world.

Now, if there were stock to buy in this company, wouldn't we buy a bundle? If this were a buried treasure, wouldn't we liquidate our assets and buy the field?[4] Too often we visualize—and act as though—God is on the opposite end of a rope trying to pull us into doing things God's way. The truth is *God and humans are on the same team!* God with tender love and yearning knows our deep desires. God knows how we ache to love and be loved; how desperately we need to be secure;

40

how aimless it is to live without purpose, meaning, fulfillment. God knows better even than we do what incredible potential lies in our beings.

God is on our side! God wants us to be loved, to be secure, to achieve, to be deeply fulfilled and met. God has put all of creation—even a member of the Godhead, Jesus—on the line to make that possible for us. It is *the* monumental lie of Satan that would deceive us into believing God's hopes and dreams are counterproductive to ours. The conflict between God and ourselves comes not from wanting different things but from thinking we know better than God how to make our dreams come true.

The instruction manual for the kingdom of God is the Gospel Order. The Gospel Order articulates those biblical principles that show us how a culture of God works. The Order is most clearly articulated in the Gospel of Matthew. However, the entire New Testament speaks to various aspects of our new adventure. In participating in the culture of God, we rejoin the heart of God. All that is God—love, power, truth, reality, life—become available to us and through us. We become the channels of God's being for a broken world.

Picture garden hoses connected to the faucet. The more fully we're connected, the more efficiently the water flows through us to the plant needing it. Our connectedness and alignment with the heart and nature of God are what release the Living Water in a situation. Our disconnection, our choosing behaviors *unlike* God's heart, turns off the flow.[5] The Gospel Order is a way to understand our participation with God.

As I see it, the run-of-the-mill Western workplace operates by world system goals, methods, and results. The financial bottom line is the goal. The methods are whatever it takes to get the most profit and still be effective and efficient. The results are a mixed bag. Some wonderful things emerge. Some dreadful things emerge. We're all recipients of both the positive and negative aspects of business in the "real" world.

On the other hand, we as God's people have a vast opportunity before us! Our workplaces—lowly, exalted, or someplace in between—are sites in which Jesus envisioned our living out the alternative system of the Gospel Order. This is the mission field for all of us who spend the greater part of our waking hours at work—or thinking about it. So what does the culture of God look like in the workplace? How do we proceed to make a difference?

Service as Ministry and Worship

Our first move to "kingdomize" our work is to understand that it is our service to God and to the world. Work is far more than a way to support ourselves and pay the bills. It is one way our lives can count. God isn't waiting for us to get situated in our perfect career—or even a job that fits us. Wherever we are we can turn our tasks into service. The very act of serving God with a heart of love becomes profound worship.

Christians throughout the centuries have known the truth about transforming their daily tasks into ministry and worship. Probably no one, however, exemplifies and tells it better than Brother Lawrence, lay brother of the Carmelites in France in the mid-1600s. He was unschooled, lame, lowly. The tasks he was assigned were those no one else wanted—including Brother Lawrence. He dreaded going to the ships to buy wine for the brothers because he was lame and the logistics of handling the casks were daunting. He had a natural aversion to kitchen duty—his primary assignment. Yet rather than resist these tasks, he embraced them in a spirit of service and worship. He is recorded as having prayed,

> Lord of all pots and pans and things . . .
> Make me a saint by getting meals
> And washing up the plates![6]

He washed each utensil. He did each task as service to his fellow humans and to God. *God* needed someone to wash the pans—and he offered his service in love of God. He did all things peaceably as acts of love and adoration.

He said that "our sanctification did not depend upon *changing* our works, but in doing that for God's sake which we commonly do for our own."[7] He explained that "the most excellent method . . . of going to God was that of doing our common business without any view of pleasing men, and (as far as we are capable) purely for the love of God.[8] This led him to conclude that

> The time of business does not with me differ from the time of prayer, and in the noise and clatter of my kitchen, while several persons are at the same time calling for different things, I possess God in as great tranquillity as if I were upon my knees at the blessed sacrament.[9]

Work that should be done in the world is work that serves. It serves a family, customers, co-workers. It serves as a link in the interdependent world. As an inventor smiles at the smooth functioning of each interlinking mechanism, so the Creator smiles as we offer up our piece of maintaining a complex world.

Does this mean that we all need to find menial labor through which to serve? Of course not. Leaders serve through the gift of their leadership abilities, their vision, their vulnerability to put themselves on the line for others. The manager is not simply resting on a rung of the ladder headed to the top. The manager serves by organizing people and tasks so folks can flourish while they accomplish the work. Skilled specialists offer their particularized gift as service to the whole. Those who support through routine and menial labor offer service as vital and noble as any other. The artists, the educators, the healers, and even the helpless all offer important gifts to the human endeavor. The measure of a person in the culture of God is not how "high" he or she has climbed in the hierarchy of jobs. It is how faithful and life-giving that person has been to the work entrusted to him or her.[10]

Queries

- Does my work serve God and humankind?
- What would I need to do to make my work a gift of love for God?
- Have I been inwardly resisting my work rather than embracing it as a gift?
- Am I angry at God for giving me this work now?
- Have I been using my work for ego, status, or survival needs rather than worship and service?
- Is there anything I need to be able to change my attitude toward my work?

Doing Love

The plumb line of a Christian's life is love. Love is holding that which is loved in authentic regard and appreciation while making choices for the well-being of what is loved. While we associate love most closely with relationships, the space of love can embrace people, things, situations—even times and places. Love holds in balance regard for ourselves as well as that which is "other" than us. This love has been the entire will of God from Genesis to Revelation, from the foundation of Creation to the end of eternity. The criterion upon which it is decided whether we're God's people rests not on correct doctrine, sacraments, or religious fervor. It rests solely on love.[11]

Jesus was clear and emphatic throughout his entire ministry. His last plea to his disciples before he was arrested was to remember the singular obedience from which all other obediences flow—love everyone. God. Yourself. Friends and kin. Brothers and sisters in Christ. Acquaintances. Strangers. Enemies. Those below us. Those above us. Those in competition with us. The helpless and marginalized. The rich and famous. Those who are wrong. Those who are evil. Those who are dangerous. Those who have or will take advantage of us. Those who owe us money or have harmed our property. Those who are not trustworthy. Those who are even despicable. Those who apparently have no bearing on our lives. Those who seem to have everything and need nothing from us. Everyone. All the time. There are no time-outs from love.

Love in the workplace flows from service and worship. If we position ourselves in an attitude of working as an act of love, then it's a small step to use love's methods in all of our interactions. Love doesn't mean *liking* everyone. Love doesn't mean ceasing to use our common sense about people and situations. Love doesn't mean turning the workplace into a fuzzy-headed hug-in. Love means taking into account the other persons involved in every action; it means acting and deciding in favor of their well-being.

For instance, if I'm making a product, love dictates that I not do sloppy work that causes a defect. It's not love to create or distribute a defective product. Love means not producing, making available, or profiting from products that harm people. If I'm dealing with a surly customer, love calls me to look beyond the infuriating nonsense to serve the person who needs.

If I'm part of an office, a team, a group of laborers—love asks me to hold each in care and respect and to make decisions "for" them. That may mean working extra to make sure the next shift has what's needed; finding constructive ways to solve problems so every team member can flourish; living into tough love that holds·another accountable; saying "no" to the person who has no sense of boundaries. It may require caring about the whole person rather than the work-doer. Love is a complex business. It has many faces. But you can recognize it because it genuinely takes account of everyone—and genuinely works for all.

Love is interesting stuff. It makes us feel wonderful. It brings us life and energy. We actually know that it makes us look more attractive and vibrant. Love is the most attractive quality in the universe. The adage that everyone loves a lover is true. When we love, we become winsome human beings. We like the way we feel inside. People like the way we are.

So God's good advice to stay in love all the time should be analogous to telling us to have dessert three times a day to stay healthy. It should strike us as totally good news. Respecting is so much more enjoyable than disrespecting a person. Finding the place to love and be for a person is a lot more fun than becoming embroiled in anger and irritation. Riding out a rough situation with a clear heart is healthier than getting dragged under by the woundedness and weaknesses of others. Being part of the solution rather than one more part of the problem helps us sleep at night. This is no poison pill that God is prescribing for us. This is the key to Life and Health and Power. Love.

Queries

- Is my work contributing to the well-being of others?
- Is my service, product, or artistic expression leading people to their best selves?
- Do the processes and procedures I use in my work honor and care for others?
- Are the conditions I create or participate in health-giving to users and workers alike?
- Are the methods I use in creation, production, advertising, marketing, selling, and servicing consistent with love?
- Are any areas of my work illegal or unethical?
- Does my work exploit anyone in the process of making a profit?
- Is there anyone in the chain of work I'm forgetting to love?

Being Authentic

Be real. God is Reality. When we're out of Reality, we're out of God. We've loosened the hose from the faucet when we play games with self and other. We're disconnected from God.

Life in general—and work in particular—is a jungle of inauthenticity. The cynicism of our age is nurtured in a tangle of half-truths, outright lies, manipulations, posturing. It's not deemed wise or cool to be authentic in the world system. Marketers present only those aspects of products that will seduce buyers. Tobacco companies simply shift the appeal to a different weakness when they know their product will harm bodies. Credit card companies make getting in debt easier than eating potato chips even as they know it leads millions of families into financial disaster. Managers make daily decisions to share only part of the story with employees.

Suspicion thrives like dandelions because there is no way to know if you have the true and real story. Trust is shattered. And real cooperation can never flourish unless there is trust. Employees cut bosses and co-workers off from their genuine selves. Management and labor alike are locked into not being able to admit weakness and limitations. Consequently, effective teamwork is hard to come by—for it requires folks to know each other's strengths and weaknesses and provide each other complementary interdependence.

In the culture of God it's safe to be real. It's safe to stand transparent in the presence of God. We're loved, treasured, forgiven. Our messes are being transformed into something useful. Our weaknesses are an occasion for God to work on our behalf and be glorified. Our strengths are empowered and liberated. We don't have to hide or pretend. All is well.

And what is well on the inside can also be well on the outside. We don't need all those walls and shields that we lug around for protection. We can face our tasks with a new sense of release. We bring who and what we are to each task. Where we need help, we can become clear and seek the assistance required. We don't have to pretend to be smarter or dumber, more or less able than we are. It is safe for the real us to come to work.

Authenticity with others in the workplace means being the same on the outside as on the inside. We voluntarily lay down the weapons of manipulation. We tell the truths of our day—and have the courage to let God flow through the conduits of our faithfulness. We let ourselves be seen—and greet others with the eyes of God when we see them. Folks are telling us who they are all the time. Now we can truly let ourselves see—for in seeing we will not be blown away or helpless. We now can afford to really see and hear what people are because we can bring the Love of God to bear on the frailty and horror of their disconnections too.

Authenticity is countercultural in today's workplaces. Often the short-term consequences of being real do give us pause. Yet in my experience, this is one of the more needed kingdom principles in the world of businesses and organizations. There are tremendous advantages to authenticity in the workplace.

• *People trust you.* Trust is created. All work is done in a web of interconnection. Trust is the basic glue of business. When you think about it, the amount of trust we put in each other and the system is astounding. A simple act of banking, for instance, involves layers and layers of trust. Authenticity makes trust possible and durable. Any organization that has trust will succeed. Trust is the gold standard of the universe.

• *Your voice is taken seriously.* If people trust you, they listen to you. Many of the games of work are held in place because people seem untrustworthy. Simply working without layers of gaming yields great energy savings, not to mention fun. A personal example: as administrator I didn't pad my budgets to protect myself from "inevitable" cuts from above. The budget projections I put on the table were realistic, economical estimates of what it would take to do the job well. As a consequence, my budgets were rarely if ever tampered with. If all budgets were submitted with the same authenticity, an entire layer of the budget process could often be eliminated.

• *Real problems can be solved.* Much time is wasted in organizations because we solve the wrong problems. Authenticity in the workplace allows us quickly to identify areas that need attention and to solve real problems with real solutions.

Inauthenticity means making decisions in a fog. Much time, effort, and emotion are wasted.

There are countless examples. How many times has your organization made a new rule, a new procedure that complicates everyone's life because one person abused the job environment? The real problem is that one worker who is seldom consulted, heard, or held accountable. Instead, blankets of procedures smother folks who need no constrictions. Often we never even know why the person deviated in the first place. There could be valuable information there if we asked!

• *Personal well-being is enhanced.* I have no studies or documentation to support that assertion. I only know from years of personal experience and counseling that many benefits are released when we stop playing games with ourselves and others. Sometimes the healing results are startling; sometimes there is increased joy and creativity. In other cases, the benefit is simply having a quiet peace with one's self.

• *Ultimately folks who are trusted prosper.* Quakers and fair pricing offer a historical example. In the 1600s, bartering was the system of England. A shrewd barterer could come home from the market with a far better deal than a child sent out for an errand. Quakers thought the Gospel Order demanded integrity and authenticity. They created the pricing system North Americans are used to. They reasoned there was a fair price for both the buyer and the seller—and integrity required charging all buyers the same price. In the early years Quakers were boycotted and derided for this unusual insistence on authenticity. But over time, Quaker shops were sought out and prospered. Folks liked knowing they were being treated fairly—and did business accordingly. This eventually changed the face of commerce in many parts of the world.[12]

Queries
• Do I accomplish my work with authenticity?
• Are the seeming demands of my work in conflict with

the integrity of who I am?
- Are there areas of my life in which I need healing so I can truly know I'm safe in the love of God?
- When have I taken chances on authenticity and found that things turned out all right?

Resting as Obedience

We live in a culture that honors extremes. Our sports heroes stretch past reasonable expectations, playing with broken bodies. We love the Mother Teresas, the Donald Trumps. We've made workaholism a national norm. We feel shamed and inadequate if we actually are rested as we work and live. It's considered an American virtue to pack more into a day than is feasible. And it's an honorable death to die of stress-related conditions.

The Gospel Order reflects a different vision of the admirable life. Gospel life is life that mirrors the God of Creation. Life that is orderly. That is measured. That includes rhythms of night and day, of summer and winter, of toil and rest. Gospel life has texture. There is both sorrow and joy, concern and celebration, beginnings and endings, yes and no.

So the concept that resting is part of obedience to God has been woven into the very fabric of Judaism and Christianity. Only in recent times have we discarded this beautiful gift as archaic and restricting. And never before has the need for the obedience of rest been more important.

The Sabbath principle—resting one day in seven—is a gift to every human. God understands that humans need a hedge against endless toil that kills body and spirit. God knows families and friends need time for play, rest, conversation. God senses that the heart needs time to commune and be with God in worship and in praise. God knows that sometimes we just need to lie down and take a nap. The world will not give us those luxuries. It will use us up and spit us out. God, who loves us, has made holy space for us always to have the joy of rest.

I'm fortunate. I have many memories of Sabbath joys. My grandparents treated Sunday legalistically. You couldn't do this and you couldn't do that. They kept the letter of their law, but they missed God's loving intent. My parents, on the other hand, seemed intuitively to understand what a gift this was. For most of my childhood, we were poor. My folks worked multiple jobs to keep us fed and clothed. But no matter how grueling the week might be, we could count on Sunday. Work would be put aside. Concerns over finances would be shelved. There was time for worship and long conversations about God, life, and plain old stuff. Over came the friends. Out came the games. Long afternoon excursions were in order. And sometimes those inevitable, dreaded naps might happen. But I could count on the family being fully present to one another. I knew that whatever the disciplines of the week, there would be a day for us.

Somehow in this context I understood—long before the thoughts formed in my mind—that God was *for* us.[13] That God loved life with us. A God day was a day of joy. When I reflect on things my folks did right, this always comes to the forefront. Sunday was an anchor in a world of delayed gratification. Sunday kept my folks healthy during times of severe stress. And I know my parents never missed an assignment or deadline because of that day of rest. God and joy became deeply associated in my consciousness.

One of my favorite memories of my daughters is of when one of their neighborhood friends surprised me by inquiring if she could join our family. As I explored this unexpected request, she explained that she wanted to belong to a family that didn't have to work on Sunday. She knew a good deal when she saw it!

And so it is. The Sabbath principle for Israel was an experience of trust. The Sabbath was not only a weekly event; the rhythm of six parts work to one part rest formed the basis of the national calendar of six years work and one year rest. In small ways we trust God to make us as productive in our six days of work as we would have been in seven. In large ways, Israel experienced the same miracle of trust that six years of crops would meet the needs of a nation that rested on the seventh.[14]

Not everyone can structure work to have Sundays off. However, this needn't mean ignoring the principle of rest. People can creatively set aside their own days of rest. All of us need to find substantial blocks of time to set apart and protect as God-time. Such time is devoted to restoration of spirit, body, and relationships. It is a break from anxiety and an investment in joy. In our fast-paced world, nothing may seem more impractical or farfetched. And nothing pays greater dividends in health, productivity, relationships, and personal well-being.

Queries

- How do I feel pulled between my work and my family and friends?
- How might I restructure my life for a Sabbath?
- What strokes do I get from people for being over-worked and tired?
- What support from my community would I need if I tried to live a more balanced life of rest and work?

Celebrating

Celebration is akin to the Sabbath principles. It is more good news that God wove into the fabric of the universe. I've always been amazed and delighted that God's people had festivals, plays, feasting, gift-giving, and play-acting all embedded in the Law.[15] Days and celebrations have changed, but the themes of celebration endure. Celebrations are part of the glue of community life. We may decry commercialism of contemporary holidays; still, such times help us transcend individualism by sharing common themes and commitments. We give ourselves to public emotion—whether the gladness and generosities of Christmas and Hanukkah or Easter's pilgrimage from sorrow to joy.

Celebration is an important component in the life of any community. Most of the Christian community adopted the First Day, Sunday, as its day of celebration. The celebration inherent in Sundays-well-kept is experienced in the change of pace that accompanies this day different than all others. The community of the workplace also needs to have the glue of celebration. Celebrations usually require planning; truthfully, great celebrations require much work, resources, time. But if authentically connected to the life of the community, celebrations also become an unseen glue of a successful workplace.

Many a company tries to celebrate. And it often fails to accomplish much. Celebration must have the following elements to be meaningful in the life of a group.

1. *Celebration must honor an actual communal event.* It can be a communal success—like overcoming great difficulties as a team, reaching a company goal, rejoicing in special achievements that make everyone's work life better, remembering a heroic part of the company's history. The greatest pitfall to such events is that one must be sure the joy is actually shared! I've seen many a party meant to be a celebration. The food was first-class. The ingredients of a party were all there. But the event was sullen because the success was good for some of the workers and painful for others. Celebrating a positive bottom line achieved on backs of exploited employees will not a party make! A problem with workplace celebrations is that management usually makes space for the party—and managers often celebrate from their vantage point. It is a wise manager who can grasp the real points of workplace pride and accomplishment.

The same principle applies when entering the dicey world of honoring some workplace achievements over others. Recently I was having dinner with a wise administrator of a college. He had just completed a miraculous overhaul of a campus. The buildings were functional in the smallest details; the grounds were lovely. One member of our dinner party noticed no paths of beaten dirt crossed the campus—instead, the lawns were a beautiful part of the landscape.

"How do you do that?" she asked. "I didn't see any signs telling students to stay off the grass."

Smiling, the president explained. When the landscaping was being planned, he took a ride in one of the cherry pickers used in construction. He noted all the paths students had made by crisscrossing the campus. He had them marked. They became the sidewalks. Clearly his strategy worked. He had capitalized on what was already functional—offering joy and beauty to all.

The same wisdom applies to the art of celebration in the workplace. Find a way to get an overview of the way your company works. See where the natural celebrations and joys are occurring. Capitalize on what is real and authentic—and it will be a joy and beauty to all.

2. *The celebration must be in meaningful currency.* A practical faux pas illustrates what I mean by this. At one point in my work history I had a boss who really valued celebrations. But they usually fell flat, and folks responded sullenly. Why? He would work his team hard. Long hours. Overwhelming tasks with difficult time lines. Achieving his goals would put the ongoing, regular work of our day way behind. We'd have to work longer and longer into the evening, come in on weekends, and take many tasks home to both fulfill the urgent ongoing tasks that never ceased *and* meet his goals.

When the goal was reached, he loved to throw a party. And he loved to "free" us from our work to have the party in the afternoon. What he never figured out was that this only put us farther behind. Now we had to stay longer at work to make up for the party. Currency that would have blessed and made us dance would have been gift certificates for two to a wonderful restaurant or free passes for the family at the local amusement park, ice follies, or circus. Or better yet, an extra bonus day of vacation.

3. *Celebrations require interruption of the routine.* Some celebrations are based on role reversal. When bosses become line workers and line workers become bosses. When employees give parties for customers, managers, or colleagues in the field. When college presidents sleep in the dorms and pull an all-nighter. Some celebrations simply alter the routine. Everyone dresses down, or wears a certain color, or creates a theme. Flowers or gag gifts and cards of appreciation show up on folks' desks and work stations. Some celebrations include skits or wondrously creative roasts, spoofs, and monologues.

Most celebrations include food—food that is fun and brings a smile. Food can alter circumstances by being out of place—as when backpackers include goblets and fine china on their mountain treks. Or food can be playful and set a mood. Or be a regional favorite that pleases the heart. Food can bless through role reversals of the servers. So ordering in pizza for one of those long, long meetings may be a nice gesture for an office that needs some celebration—but having a fine meal with china delivered unexpectedly during those working meetings sets a whole different tone in the joy of collaboration and hard work.

It isn't our normal pattern to think of celebration as part of the Gospel Order. But Jesus' life is filled with celebration. His first recorded miracle took place at a marriage celebration.[16] Jesus was a full participant in the celebratory cycles of the Jewish festivals. When we read about his reticence to heal the Syrophonecian woman while they were at the coastal towns of Tyre and Sidon, we can even surmise that he and the disciples took a vacation.[17] The images of final restoration of the kingdom in Revelation end with one of the most joyous of celebrations, the wedding feast. Celebration seems to be the nature of the Eternal Restoration. We live in a world that knows so little of joy that it equates partying with getting obliterated by alcohol. The Gospel Order is gift that helps us be alive, vibrant, productive, and joyful.

Queries

- What are places in my life of faith, family, and work that deserve celebration?
- What are ways I can cultivate a more celebratory spirit?
- What stands in the way of my being fully present to celebration?

DISCUSSION QUESTIONS

1. How are the the world's system and God's different?

2. Why is the world system sometimes so tempting?

3. The Sermon on the Mount presents the Gospel Order in a nutshell. Discuss how the Sermon is an instruction manual for a successful life.

4. What is true success? What are markers of its presence?

5. If God were right now writing your epitaph, what would it say? What would you like God to write?

Part Two

PITFALLS AND PROCESS

4

Control

When we don't trust God, *we* have to take control. We have to control anything and everything to try to stay safe. When something slips out of our control, we're driven to increasingly bizarre thoughts and behaviors to reach the illusory goal of safety. We control because we've become our own gods. Not very good gods, mind you—but gods nevertheless.

As soon as we even begin to contemplate immigrating into the kingdom of God through our work, the gods of control huff and puff to blow our house down. Westerners are control freaks because we've made ourselves centers of the universe. Because that's an unnatural and impossible position, it saps incredible energy. So we exhaust ourselves while squandering amazing gifts of God's love. Stress, burnout, anger, and fear are natural by-products of control.

Work is the most visible focal point in the struggle to control life. Work is the scepter of our false god. To talk in new ways about work is to battle Mammon itself.[1] So before we can see the possibilities of the Kingdom come here as in Heaven, we must face the dragons of control.

Control is the act of making things turn out all right through our efforts. The opposite of control is trust. We were built for trust. That's the way our bodies, minds, and spirits were designed. Actually when trust is complete we're eternal beings. Everything works smoothly—infinitely. You can feel the difference right now. Look away from this book. Feel all the tensions in your body. Now take a deep breath and feel the safe, warm love of God all around and through you. Amazing physical difference, isn't it? Losing trust in God's love didn't simply rupture relationships. It sabotaged our bodies and our psyche—making us finite.

Salvation is a commitment to trust Jesus to save us. Save us from what? Our sins, naturally. But what are our sins? They're not the laundry list of behaviors. Our sins are all the ways we futilely try to control rather than trust. The behaviors are simply fruit of the wild-goose chase of control. These behaviors are destructive and painful because control is the opposite of trusting God. God has come to us to save us from ourselves. To save us from the futile need to spend ourselves in pursuit of safety through control.

When we're saved we start the rebuilding process. It's rather like the image of living in a war-ravaged village. Brick by brick, building by building we restore things to the original beauty of trust. God's Spirit dwells in us to take all the same old stuff of life—and rebuild it in new patterns. The blueprint is God's love. Work is the brick and trust the mortar.

Dragons of Control

Every time we start to trust God, the dragons of control belch fire at us. Here are predictable messages.

• *Your work defines your worth.* If you have an important job, you are an important person. If you have a lowly job, you are a lowly person. If you don't have work, you have lost your worth.

• *Work gives you income, and income keeps you safe.* Money—and what money can buy—is what keeps the pain of life at bay.

• *Life is a ladder.* The higher up you are, the safer. You get higher by getting more power, prestige, wealth, status. Your purpose in life is to get as high as you can.

• *Work is a battlefield.* Everyone needs control—and is battling for it. So it's important always to be on top, to keep an edge. If you're not number one, you're vulnerable. If you're number one today, you must keep on your toes because someone will unseat you tomorrow.

- Nobody likes a loser. Love goes to the winners.
- God wants us to be winners for him.
- God expects us to do the work.

Trust, the Dragon Slayer

The culture of God doesn't play by these rules. Trust's maxims are different.

- *Trust defines your worth.* The child who trusts naturally is the most important person.[2] An example of this redefinition is seen in the story of Jesus and the Roman centurion in Capernaum. In a system of control, the centurion's position in society would trump a wandering teacher's position. But the centurion understood the kingdom of God. He was the one beseeching Jesus. He trusted that Jesus was connected to God. "Only say the word, and my servant will be healed." Jesus was impressed! He hadn't seen faith—or trust—like this in all Israel. "I tell you, many will come from east and west and sit at table with Abraham and Isaac." The seats of honor are reserved for those who trust.[3]

- *God provides for all your needs.* Like birds and flowers, your care isn't actually a product of your making. It's a gift of God.[4]

- *Life is a marriage.* Circumstances come and go. Life has cycles. Joys and sorrows. Pleasures and pains. Strengths and weaknesses. Births and deaths. God "has made everything beautiful in its time; also he has put eternity into man's mind."[5] Not the events but the relationships define life.[6]

- *Work is a battlefield.* It's the arena in which light overcomes darkness and good defeats evil. Work is a Lamb's War.[7] The guileless, the peaceful, the servant enter the world of work and transforms it from death to life. Service replaces control—and Life flourishes. Love replaces competition—and prosperity flows. The first support the last—and all succeed.[8]

• *Love is a unique gift to every human.* God loves us just the way we are. God enjoys our strengths. God is glorified by our weaknesses.[9] God's love sorrows deeply when we shoot ourselves in the foot through mistrust and wrong choosings. But God doesn't cease to love us dearly and passionately. God doesn't love us in some dispassionate, universal way that ignores our specific personhood. As each of our friendships are unique creations of two distinct persons, so our friendships with God are distinct and special. The God who grasps the totality of the cosmos also cherishes the freckle on our nose.[10]

• *God simply wants one thing of us—our love.* Love that turns its heart to God and leaps with joy and anticipation. Love that looks at what God loves—and joins the river of goodness. In the culture of God, work is an act of love. It's a natural fruit of our being. Love adores serving. And so we do. Serve God. Serve our fellow humans. Serve our wonderful world.

• *God lets us join God and the heavenly hosts in the work.* Work is a privilege. It's a joy of our heart. It accomplishes God's purposes on earth.

The Way Forward

Know that the most hotly contested battles for your trust will be fought in the arena of the workplace. This stronghold of the world system is heavily guarded. If there is a place it's hard to believe God is sovereign and trustworthy, it's work. This false god doesn't give in easily. And when financial fears nip at our heels and howl at our doors, it's hard not to try to serve both Mammon and God. Like the Israelites who sneaked up to the groves to worship the fertility deities, just in case, we like to play the "and too" game also. Yet we know the words. "You shall have no other gods before me."[11] "No one can serve two masters."[12]

So we draw a line in the sand and commit our life of work to God. We take it down from its pedestal and lay it at the feet of our Lord and King. No longer do we serve it. No longer do we come at its beck and call. It's a rightful part of our life that serves the God of glory. This is a major reorientation to life in our society. The logistics of work may remain the same, but the attitude about the work changes. New questions and issues, new challenges and joys arise. And this reorientation enrolls us in the best retirement plan in the universe!

Big decisions and commitments are important. They're markers on our road of life. But the journey is then made in all the million little decisions along the way. I can intend to go from Seattle to New York City. I can pack the car and set out to do so with great resolve. But if I fail to keep making the decisions to stay on the highways leading to New York, I may end up in Galveston despite good intentions. Likewise, staying in the culture of God may start with a decisive commitment, but the journey is made choice by choice by choice.

Thomas Kelly and Frank Laubach were Christians able to articulate how we align ourselves with God in the choices of the moment.[13] They expressed it differently, but both understood that we live on two levels of consciousness. On one level we go about our regular business. We're fully attentive to whatever is before us. But just underneath we're also conscious of God's loving presence. We carry an inner image of God's nature. And we keep the two levels consonant.

It's like focusing a camera. We look at the image. If it's fuzzy and unclear, we keep focusing until what we see is what we wish to photograph. Likewise we look at the choice in front of us and decide what matches God's heart. And work performed in the presence of God is work well done.

How do we *do that*? Frank Laubach explains:

> Thinking is a process of talking to your "inner self." Instead of talking to yourself, talk to the Invisible Christ. If you do that all

day every day, then your thoughts are spreading Christ all over the planet wherever other minds are tuned in to yours. Hundreds of thousands, or perhaps millions, of minds will be better.[14]

All during the day *in the chinks of time* between the things we find ourselves obliged to do, there are moments when our minds ask: "What next?" In these chinks of time, ask Him: "Lord, think Thy thoughts in my mind. What is on Thy mind for me to do now?" When we ask Christ, "What next?" we *tune in* and give Him a chance to pour His ideas through our enkindled imagination. If we persist, it becomes a habit. It takes some effort, but it is worth a million times what it costs. It is possible for *everybody, everywhere*. Even if we are surrounded by throngs of people we can continue to talk silently with our invisible Friend. We need not close our eyes nor change our position nor move our lips.[15]

At first this may sound tedious. Like any skill, it takes practice. But it's more natural than it first sounds. Consider being in love: we carry out regular tasks—but something's different. In the corner of our mind we now see everything in light of what our beloved thinks and feels. We smile as we remember a shared joke. We have new concerns. We have added perspectives. We feel different inside because we carry love and our beloved within. This new orientation to life is really just the same thing. We carry love and our Beloved within.

Now when we live each moment in conversation with the Invisible Christ, our control needs wither. It's a natural process. We don't need to wrest power away from anyone because we're participating in the ocean of light and love. We're part of the river of righteousness flowing abundantly over the earth. We're ultimately safe, liberated from self-absorption, free, home. We're in a flow of being that lasts forever.

This inner conversation informs us about the practical acts of our lives. We know when to take initiative and when to sit back and watch. We know when to labor long and when to rest. We know how to tap into creativity and wisdom. We know how to proceed—because the inner conversation informs us as we go. We won't necessarily know what to do about tomorrow or five years from now, but we *will* know what to do now. And in being obedient to now, we'll know the next step.[16]

DISCUSSION QUESTIONS

1. What do we mean when we say that someone is controlling?

2. What are the differences between leadership and control? Between power and control? Sovereignty and control?

3. What would tempt me to serve the master of work?

4. What things have helped us keep Jesus in all our thought? How do we know what God is communicating with us in the inner conversation?

5. How do we stay safe if we aren't controlling things?

Fear

The natural consequence of control is fear. Control is a makeshift solution to our need for security. Our ability to control depends on many factors, including how competent and strong we are; how well we control those around us; how much we control the realms beyond our fingertips as nature, nations, disease, history, the future. No matter how much control of ourselves and circumstances we manage, no matter how great a hedge we put between ourselves and an unpredictable outer world, much remains beyond our control. So there will always be something to fear.

Fear is the psychological and physiological barricade around pain and danger. Since the Fall, fear has been a natural feature of the human psyche. Fear can be a friend by marking dangers—giving us adequate opportunity to have that inner conversation with God that, in turn, gives us wisdom to proceed. In the life of a trust-filled person, fear is sometimes present but not dominant. But fear is the constant companion of those focused on maintaining control.

Fear actually escalates as we take more control. I've a friend who wanted to be financially secure to be free from childhood uncertainties. He was delightfully successful. So he bought the things that go with having enough. Among those things was an expensive dream car. Then he realized his car put him in danger. His car could entice thieves. Worse, he could be followed home and danger would know where he lived. Now his home and family were vulnerable. So he bought a gun to protect the very things that were to protect him from insecurity. He developed a guardedness as he continually scanned the environment and even acquaintances for threats. His control had brought no rest.

So it always is. Control leads to fear. The better we are at control, the more we fear. Control is one of the crueler of life's wild-goose chases.

Thus it stands to reason that Westerners who have so much to be secure about are fearful. Messages of fear surround us. We spend a disproportionate amount of our income on insurances. The media is saturated with news of what to fear today. It's fascinating to watch the growing web of fear being created all around us.

I suppose it has always been true that we've feared the unknown, the stranger, the mysterious. But now we're being conditioned to fear those close to us—parent, child, neighbor, friend. We've become so terrified of dying that we fear our own bodies, the food we eat, the air we breathe. We've tried to control our environment so totally that weather reports raise fear over a downpour of rain or whitewash of snow.

The workplace too is saturated with fear. Fear about ourselves and others. Fear in the guise of competition. Fear of what the powers that be are doing. Fear of what our co-workers aren't doing. Fear about the future.

Scripture says much about fear. At first glance the Bible seems constantly to contradict itself. Passage after passage exhorts folks to fear the Lord. Then repeatedly God tells people to fear not. Intuitively we understand the paradox, though we may find it hard to verbalize. The biblical text is stressing that folks fear a lot of things. But there is really only one thing in the universe worthy of fear. God is the only force to be reckoned with.

In a world where God is discarded as a swear word or an irrelevant idea, it's still important news that of all the things humans worry about only one should concern us: God. The fear of God is the beginning of wisdom.[1] But it isn't the end of it! The end of fear is the other side of the coin: perfect love casts out fear.[2] When we take God seriously love melts fear. The danger departs; the barricades can come down.

What rightfully remains is a knowledge of reverence and awe. The mystery we live into on a daily basis is that the God who is our reckoning is the same God who shares with us as friend and beloved. The day we lose the wonder of this is the day we need to be reminded to fear the Lord. The gift we hold is exceedingly precious. Never trivialize the privilege of living in God's presence.

At the same time, we've been granted the run of the universe. We can run and play and work and be with the same childlike abandon of little John-John Kennedy playing in the Oval Office. God hasn't asked us to tiptoe around the kingdom in a spirit of timidity. The saints of my childhood had it right when they reminded us to "come boldly to the throne of grace." We're being made into co-heirs with Christ.[3] Wow. That is some generosity! With that going for us, how can we be afraid? Or in the words of Paul, "If God is for us, who is against us?"[4]

Work without Fear

In light of this, what are the implications for being God's person in the workplace? As we're learning not to be shackled by the fears of the world, we find new reference points.

We've a new boss

In the kingdom of God, Jesus is our boss.[5] The inner conversation with the Invisible Christ becomes the backbone of our work. When there is no conflict between the intentions and methods of Jesus and the work we're doing, we're to serve through our work as if serving Jesus—because we are. If we're in positions of teaching or leadership, Jesus models our style. We use leadership and power to serve and bless. If we're supporting others, we do our work as if Jesus is our visible employer or customer. We answer the phone as if Jesus is on the other end. We create, market, and service products as if Jesus is the consumer.

We're familiar with the simple genius of Mother Teresa. She became admired simply by superimposing the face of Jesus on every person she encountered. So she tended to the sick and dying street people of India with the same tenderness and reverence with which she would have ministered to the literal Son of God. Her amazing courage, wisdom, and accomplishments all rose from that singular practice of doing every action for, with, and unto Jesus.

Now sometimes what we're asked to do conflicts with the heart of God. When conflicts arise, God needs to win. If Jesus wouldn't buy it, we don't make it or sell it. Several years ago the monotony of a cross-country flight was broken by a fascinating conversation with a military engineer. It became apparent our lives were working in different directions. I was a Quaker theologian and teacher. He was a designer of armament.

As we deplaned in single file, he said to me, "Please pray to God that we never use what I make!"

As folks surged between us, the moment for conversation was lost. Only in my mind was I able to respond, "I pray to God that you stop making what you make."

We're responsible not to make things that are technically possible but morally wrong. If Jesus is our boss, we walk away from situations that don't honor God and carry out *God's* purposes on the earth.

Trust lets the chips fall where they may.

God is providing for us

We can afford to do work congruent with God's purposes because in God's kingdom our survival doesn't depend on our work. Jesus is clear that God has every intention of taking fine care of us.[6] God's intention since the beginning of time has been to care for us. The Covenant promise reiterated all through Scripture is that "I will be your God and you will be my people." God didn't mean that in some pie-in-the-sky, spiritual way. God meant that the crops would bear their harvest, children live and prosper, life be long and healthy, nations be secure and peaceful. God knows what we want and intends to bless us with goodness.

We can take encouragement from communities of faith that have stood for right and have prospered. The stories are rich and abundant. In my tradition we have many wonderful historical witnesses of God's care. *Friends in Science and Industry* chronicles the most comprehensive movement of losing jobs for principles.

Early Quakers found themselves out of work for a host of reasons. Their refusal to participate in war kept them from military careers or from occupations that supplied the military. Their refusal to pay tithe to what they considered to be the corrupt Anglican Church landed them in jail on a regular basis. This meant they could not be farmers or merchants because they weren't there to tend to the crops, and their merchandise was constantly being taken as payment. They couldn't be in the professions that required good standing in the Anglican Church. So education, law, and medicine were areas not readily available to them.

In the early years of the Quaker movement, 30,000 Friends were displaced from their jobs by the constraints of their convictions. Yet in a generation they became amazingly prosperous. Because of their unquestioned integrity and honesty, the banking industry became their forte. Barclay Bank and Lloyd's of London are ensuing establishments that ring a bell with us today.

New inventions and businesses flourished. The Darby family, for one, invented new uses for iron—and iron pots and pans were created. Iron bridge works were created. New foundry techniques were developed. Quaker convictions took them into educational reform, prison reform, care for the mentally ill. Their hardships propelled them to the Colonies, where they were pioneers of political theory and practice. The cost of discipleship changed the circumstances of their lives but didn't separate them from God's abundant love and care.[7]

There are limitless possibilities

We're vulnerable to fear when we can't see how things are going to work out. Evil's most effective trick is to delude us into thinking we're in a no-win situation. The truth of the transformations in the kingdom of God is that every circumstance can become useful for us and for life. We're never trapped. We never have to be hapless victims.

We may not like or choose the process, but if we persist in trust and alignment with the heart of God, all things will work together for good. Joining God's heart connects us to the infinite, opening us to solutions and ways forward we'd never have dreamed or schemed. There is nothing more adventuresome and rewarding than life with God!

Waiting in the face of fear

Our fears tempt us to bail out before the transformation is complete. I'm reminded of a caterpillar that breaks out of the claustrophobic constraints of the cocoon and never gets to know the joy of being the butterfly. Waiting through the process of transformation is a tender time. There are several temptations to avoid while waiting.

1. Taking matters in our own hands. If we break the flow and try to save things by taking control, we make a mess. We get the pain we were afraid of. We short-circuit the work of God. Like Abraham and Sarah, we do an Ishmael; then we have to live with unintended consequences of our ineptness.[8]

2. Leaving God's love to blame, punish, pay back. We can't have it both ways. We can't both trust God to do some-

thing wonderful *and* make someone else pay for causing the situation. Leaving the heart of God breaks the transforming process and leaves us again on our own.

3. Trying to have hope. Many a person has crashed and burned in the glider of hope. We shift our focus from the face of God to hoping for a given outcome. This puts wind in our sails for a while—but if what we picture doesn't materialize quickly, we plummet. Then we find ourselves left with more hopeless pain than we faced in the original tension of waiting. Folks lose their faith not because trusting God's love fails but because they lost hope in an outcome or expectation.

4. Avoiding cynicism. When the wait's long and painful, it's easy to just whittle down our expectations and become cynical. This is deadly for the spirit and the body. "Lord, help my unbelief" may be a "momently" prayer for those tempted to cynicism.

Waiting in the face of fear calls for a special space in the human spirit. This doesn't come naturally to most of us. I'd describe it as a patient stillness that continues to look out and love God and others. Enduring with a gentle open spirit. Surrendering all the temptations, plans, and schemes that rise up in us to solve the "problem." Following the leadings of the inner conversation with our Lord.

There are many work problems you or I can't solve. These situations involve not abstract woes but real people, hardships, frustrations that make days stressful. They take a real toll on emotions, health, and quality of life. If we're not part of the kingdom, it's wise to fear in such circumstances. But as part of the family of God, we have the privilege and the power to be part of this transformation process. What a wonderful gift we can give our work.

We practice small steps of trust

Trust doesn't come all at once. It's built in increments. Judaism was brilliantly constructed to incorporate small steps of trusting Yahweh into the ordinary fabric of the Hebrew life. The Sabbaths were weekly experiences of trusting God with time. The weekly habits of fasting gave confidence that there indeed are invisible realities as sustaining as food and drink. The tithes were practical ways to support ministry; they were also avenues for trusting God's care financially. The mass migration of adult males to Jerusalem for the celebration of the Passover was a powerful experience of trusting God for the protection of loved ones and national security.

We're wise to practice trust in small things. For we do in a crisis what we've done in the small print of our lives. If we've practiced blessing co-workers each time our feelings hurt, then we'll have little trouble staying in the space of love when our situation looks bleak. If we've practiced talking to God about the details of our job, we'll be prepared to receive guidance when we must make crucial decisions. If we trust God in rush hour traffic to transform all things, we'll be in good shape when it comes to labor-management disagreements.

We don't have to face the fears of our lives alone. The community of faith is there to help us open our eyes to whatever frightens us—and meet it with the Spirit of God. Sometimes we need the prayers of God's family. Sometimes we need teaching. Often we just need someone to hold our hand. We're blessed by Scripture and the cloud of witnesses who have gone ahead of us. We're grateful for those who share their stories so we too can meet fear with transformation.

DISCUSSION QUESTIONS

1. What fears are in my workplace?
2. What Scriptures address these fears?
3. Do other temptations arise for me when I'm afraid?
4. What practical things can I do at work to melt my fears?
5. Do we share congregational fears? How might we meet them with love?

6

Anger

The most common emotion in the workplace is anger. This is natural and understandable. We experience anger when the world is not behaving the way we want and expect it to.[1] We all walk around with ideas of how things should be. We know how a clerk should act, a child respond, another driver move in traffic. We're walking encyclopedias of how anything in any situation "should" be !

Not only do we have expectations of everything and everyone, we give each expectation an urgency ranking. When we feel, sense, or believe our survival depends on having an expectation met we experience rage. When it doesn't suit our druthers, but we know that in the end all will be well, we experience irritation or frustration.

Imagine a driver entering ahead of you in bumper-to-bumper traffic. If you have plenty of time and the day is lovely, you may simply mildly ponder the driver's rudeness. But if you're late for an urgent appointment and traffic is moving at just that rate that every car length seems to count, you'll be much angrier. Or if a driver cuts in front of you on the interstate and you barely manage to avoid a deadly collision, you may feel an explosion of rage. "We could all have been killed!"

Now some people's anger is stuck in high gear. They're like a car with a wedged accelerator. Some people have experienced much pain or interpret it in such a way that everything triggers the same life-and-death response. "Yes, it may only be that dinner is late. But if dinner is late and you know I'm hungry, that says you don't really care about my needs. And if you don't care about my needs in small things, I can't count on your being there for the big things. Then you may leave me like my mother did. And I thought I'd die from the pain when she left." Logic can tell a person that every late meal doesn't signal desertion, but heart and psyche need healing before they can hear otherwise.

Anger Thrives at Work

Work is the perfect anger hothouse. It doesn't matter if you're saint or scoundrel. In fact, sainthood might increase the struggle with anger! Here's the deal. At work we all depend on others. Each unit is linked to others. If the night shift leaves work undone, it puts an extra burden on the day shift. If the supplier doesn't do the job flawlessly, the retailer has egg on the face. If the machinery malfunctions, the entire operation is in jeopardy.

Even lofty executives still depend on maintenance crews. Being higher in the pecking order doesn't mean being safe from the pain and jeopardy of interdependence. No one is totally free from it. Moving to the mountains and working solo may come close, but you still have suppliers, communities, and governance.

In any interdependent situation, each person's code of expectations go on auto pilot. The night shift should behave this way. The manager should be wise and do it this way. The supplier's common sense should tell her to do it this way. Anyone knows you have to come to work on time. On and on it goes—unless we tackle anger realistically and constructively.

The problem with anger is that even though it reveals our pain to another, it doesn't solve problems. Rather, it creates new problems on top of original ones. Picture each feeling and act of anger as a piece of garbage. Something goes amiss. Person after person senses the problem and dumps garbage on the situation. In most workplaces, the dumping doesn't end with the immediate players. Each worker then needs to tell someone about the incredibly stupid thing that has happened. So workers in other departments, friends, or relatives all add to the pile of anger. Probably the original problem won't be addressed, so the garbage will remain all around that action, person, decision, department. And tomorrow when nature takes its course and another expectation isn't met, more garbage will be dumped.

Most of our lives are littered by the unseen garbage of anger. I know institutions that simply cannot find their way forward because they have been entombed in years of anger and unforgiveness. New faces come, but nothing changes, for the anger still controls the position, office, company. When anger is institutionalized, when it has long been detached from its root pain, when it has been generalized from a specific pain to sweeping blame—we experience suspicion, cynicism, generic mistrust.

Anger can cripple a workplace by cutting both inwardly and outwardly. An angry person hopes to injure the one who has done a dirty deed. But the truth is that the energy and the adrenaline it requires to sustain the anger take an enormous toll on the angry one. Daily anger can play havoc with our health. It should be incentive enough for companies to deal with anger constructively to save health care costs!

Angry people carry anger with them. Anger not resolved in the workplace becomes a driving hazard in rush hour. It becomes a trigger for family violence. It forms the basis of a dysfunctional political system. It's ironic—but understandable in light of expectations—that North Americans who have so much are so often so angry.

Christians and Anger

We Christians are often handicapped in our effort to deal with anger. We have two strikes against us. First, we have higher expectations about ourselves and the world. This only heightens the sense of discrepancy between our internal catalog and the reality of any given day. In fact, the side effect of really having eyes to see will be anger. Then we see how very much the world is not as it "should" be. And this evokes anger. We even dodge the issue this raises by labeling it "righteous indignation" and give it permanence and power it never merited.

Second, many Christians have been taught that anger is wrong. So rather than becoming experts on meeting and dealing with anger, we've been prone to ignore or deny it. Consequently we're often walking bombs of unresolved anger. Christians, personal emissaries of God's love and forgiveness on the earth, have not understood the mission of stopping the steamroller of workplace anger.

How Do We Stop Anger?

Have a realistic view of the world

In the arena of work we've come to expect zero defects in service and products. We all enjoy the fruit of this goal. It's wonderful to know that buying a car won't generally leave us with a lemon. We count on research data to be generally accurate. We trust that many persons in authority give us complete and valid information on which to base decisions and actions. The goal of no errors is on target.

However, people don't come error-free. Everyone makes mistakes. Consider the simple, normal volume of mistakes to be expected from competent, efficient, trustworthy coworkers. If all made only one mistake a month—how many mistakes would we still have to deal with? And if folks were more like you and me—how many normal gaffes might there be in a day? Multiply that by the number of people who affect our work! That's a lot of "oops." Zero defects don't come because individuals work flawlessly. Zero errors come when we work as a team, checking and balancing each other. Quality control is the result of teamwork.

Many of us have unrealistic expectations. I unconsciously went to work day after day expecting perfect days. No mistakes by me or anyone. Good and wise decisions from every department. Congenial attitudes everywhere. Of course most days disappointed. Realistic expectations allow us to brainstorm creative and helpful solutions so all can succeed. Good work doesn't depend on unrealistic expectations that push folks to unreasonable goals. Good work results when realistic problems are met constructively. For instance, I'm working at a computer that "knows" I'm an imperfect speller in a world that expects written perfection. The discrepancy between the expectation and my ability is solved through spell-check. Win-win.

Mountains of anger could be hauled off to the dump if each of us entered the workplace with more realistic expectations of ourselves and co-workers. Then we could spend our energy on creating solutions and support systems to help us all succeed. Anger comes from failure to meet expectations. Changing expectations to problem solving dissolves many workplace angers.

Anger management is a key task for those of us who oversee work and people. How often a recurring irritant causes angers to flare. People are blamed, gossiped about, given poor evaluations, deprived of voice in the organization. They in turn become defensive and angry. They become less able to receive help or adjust their course.

Anger-based management blames, evaluates and withholds. Problem-solving management feels the irritant and understands there are solutions to explore. It's surprising at how simple most solutions can be. A different way of organizing information. A more realistic timeline. A change in flow or placement of supplies. A system for nonjudgmental quality control.

Those of us who aren't in management can still move toward problem solving. Rather than stew over the stupidity of managers, politicians, or regulations that cause us hardship, we can find out why the situation is this way. Sometimes there's a reasonable explanation for the hardship accompanying a task. More often, no one knew or thought about the problem. Our input as team player can improve the entire process. Organizations that seek regular feedback from persons doing the task will be more efficient than hierarchically structured ones. In terms of anger reduction, it's unreasonable to expect workers to move from anger to problem solving if they have avenues for making it happen.

Stop the chain reaction

Anger is a signal that something is amiss between our expectations and a situation. It's a red flag that pops up to help us pause and notice. Anger is a friend, an ally for the self-aware person. The role of anger in our lives is to signal that we need to re-look at what's happening at that moment—that there's a problem to be solved. The solution may simply require a small midcourse adjustment. Or anger may signal a larger problem that needs to be thought through and solved later. Anger may reveal a piece of ourselves that needs love and attention. It may signal that we need to make different choices. It may let us see a whole area of woundedness that needs God's healing touch. The anger itself is simply a flag that then needs to be discarded. It's a messenger to dismiss once the message is delivered!

The most common human mistake is making anger be the issue. We invite anger in as long-term guest, feeding and nurturing it, sharing it with friends, stoking it like a well-tended fire. But the fire of anger misused destroys. It chars the body and spirit of the angry one. It blowtorches relationships. It's as contagious as a match in a dry forest.

Taming angers in our lives and workplaces involves breaking common chain reactions. Take a normal scenario from a day at the office—

Crucial information is missing—again. Another horrible management decision has been made! Is there no end to the stupidity? Anger rises. You're again going to needlessly spend extra time at the office. You feel disgusted at the individual or department that has let you down.

You stand and toss papers down on your desk, then walk to the watercooler, shedding comments on secretaries and co-workers. You may make an angry phone call to tell department X what you think of their shoddy work. You may allow yourself the luxury of thumping the candy machine. Or you may put on a quiet exterior and feel that incredible headache coming. You're probably still fuming when you get home from work, where you grumpily inform folks that you had a cruddy day.

The inner stew is still bubbling—and the kids' artwork from school is brushed aside as another irritant. The phone call asking you to drop by and do an errand for Aunt Sally tips the scale. Can't anyone take care of themselves anymore? You need a break. So you settle in front of the television, zoning out until you can go to bed and rise to do it all over again.

But you don't have a fresh start the next day. You're just waiting for the knuckleheads to show their ineptness again. Your co-workers now share your indignation. Boy, it feels good to have someone on your side!

With x-ray vision into the human drama, we'd see the destruction left behind. Your body has suffered a chemical assault through the rush of emotion you provided it. Instead of allowing it only briefly to affect your body before moving on, you've allowed hours of stress to work on your precious organs. You've spread dis-ease to co-workers like an airborne virus. Now each of them has your stress to process in their bodies, psyches, families.

The target of your displeasure is heaped with mountains of disapproval, disrespect, negative vibes—which in turn diminishes that person's ability to thrive and do well. Communication and interaction become more terse. You talk less; you know less; you understand less. And you discover that when you do finally get around to problem solving and need this person's cooperation, he's of course reluctant to offer it.

Let's use imaginary instant replay. There are scores of places to break the chain reaction. A good place to start is at the beginning. The irritant is before you. You feel the anger rise. You recognize it—and take stock. What's going on here? Why aren't they giving us full information? What's the best way to proceed? A quick phone call or an informal chat to see why this is happening? A brainstorming session with the supervisor? An interdepartmental meeting? A fresh proposal?

Or perhaps the problem is with an individual who is struggling. What would help her succeed? Does she need a listening ear? Does he have everything he needs to do his work successfully? Or is he a troublemaker who enjoys anger and uproar? Or someone who routinely moves from crisis to crisis?

The point is not that everything's fine. The world is filled with ornery, dysfunctional people. Organizations don't always run on sound logic and good business principles. Not every business cares for its employees or the quality of its product. The point is that until you've identified the reality of the situation you can't become a constructive problem solver. The red flag of anger is signaling that you have a problem. Solving it is easiest at the beginning.

However, not all is lost if you let that moment slip by and hold on to the anger. There are many more chances to change course! The initial flare can be followed by a time-out. Walk *past* co-workers and give yourself a break. Everyone's work is different—but a rest room can be a useful site for re-centering! Maybe it's time to walk the memo to the other office. Check on the progress of project C. Go in your office and shut the door. Or simply find a restful, sunny beach to imagine; take a mini-vacation in your head.

The greatest gift you can give the earth at angry moments may be to refrain from sharing your emotions with those around you. And believe me, that's hard! Anger demands to be shared! "Someone should know what they did!" It feels wrong that you should have to deal with this inside when it's their fault, their mistake. So any restraint you can find at such moments is helpful. You may need to talk about it. That's okay. Have a friend or two with whom you can sort out feelings and issues. The crucial difference between constructive and destructive conversation is whether it's in the spirit of finding solutions or hurting others.

Contain the spread of anger

But let's say anger already fills you and the workplace. Feelings have swirled. Words have flown. The whirlwind is in motion. Many of us find we need a firewall between leaving work and re-entering our relationships with friends and relatives. Commuting can be a time of increasing frustration and danger *or* intentionally structured for restoration. Commutes can be a great time to talk with God, to enter into the conversations you were too preoccupied to have during the day. Music may soothe and calm the spirit. Turning your inner attention to those you will join helps you shift gears. You don't have to solve all the problems today. This way may well be able to wait.

Take time to love and appreciate yourself. Give yourself the feedback you're always hoping someone else will give you. Pay attention to your own needs. Is the back of your neck aching? Would a hot shower help ready you for the evening? Do you need fun? Would it be a playful delight to do something unexpected this evening? Do you need something you can't have? Image it and live into its joys with your heart.

Then turn focus on others. What is happening in their day? How can you be love to them? Start to anticipate the next piece of your day. Will the kids be wild and noisy while you need peace and quiet? Will your spouse be waiting with tasks and expectations when all you want is to collapse in the easy chair? Think ahead. Make a strategy. If you're clear about your needs, chances are good that they can be accommodated—or at least you can gain a sense of long-term give and take. If you think ahead to some win-win options for meeting conflicting needs, you stand a good chance of feeling good.

In any case, create habits of the mind that help you close the workday and open the rest of your life. If your work comes home with you, take a break and change the tempo before you resume grading papers or generating that brief.

Clean up your messes

Now anger sometimes surprises even us. It gets out of hand before we know what's happening. It's still not too late to be constructive. It will take longer to go back through the process and mend all the pieces. To be effective in any long-term way, the mending needs to have the following ingredients.

Responsibility and invitation. Folks can't hear you when they sense you're mad at them. The mending conversations need to start with your relating what this situation triggered in you. They may have helped precipitate the feeling, but the anger is yours. No one "makes" us angry. *Our* expectations breed the anger. They may be right, needful, even shared expectations, but they're *ours*. The mending conversation leads the discussion toward future problem solving; it needs to be in the context of all parties contributing equally toward possible solutions. There is no mending if one party simply dictates to the other. Vulnerability accompanies mending in which all parties are invited into the problem solving.

Apology and restitution. Depending on the damage done, apologies need to be given. Restitution needs to follow. The rule of thumb is this: whoever you shared the anger with must know you've apologized and that mending is going on.

There is usually an important task of restoring that person's reputation. Anger's primary weapon is the diminishment of another. Anger means to wound. It's the responsibility of the person who has spoken or acted in anger to restore any damaged reputation. You tarnished it; you fix it. Be as public or private in your reconciliation as you were in your anger.

Share the credit. Share the credit and the joy of reconciliation. Any solving of conflict is a credit to all parties. Be inclusive and generous in the aftermath.

Love the enemy

Love isn't some ethereal feeling that wafts around the workplace. It's the hardheaded, practical, specific care God gives us for every human on earth. If we're waiting for warm, fuzzy feelings for everyone, the wait will be long and futile.

The world is filled with folks who will cause us pain and loss. Not everyone is nice or kind or cares a hoot about the well-being of others. Some folks are so solidified in their self-orientation that they become truly evil.

But the love that comes from God's heart cares about the well-being of the other. Such love doesn't always please a person. It doesn't mean we never say "no." It certainly doesn't require dropping our own needs and desires simply to be whipped around by others' woundedness. It does mean doing everything to take the other person's well-being into account. Such love is cautious about any action that will harm another. It walks extra miles to lessen any harm that may be necessary.

The miracle of Christianity is enacted when we step over the line and include our enemies in our goodness and care. Now Christians have a clever way of ignoring the central command of Christ to love our enemies. We bat our spiritual eyelashes and say, "*I don't have any enemies.*" But the truth is that we have scores of enemies.

Enemies are those who are set against our best interests, who seek to harm us. You don't have to be a bad person to be an enemy. In fact, most enemies aren't bad at all. They're simply persons, groups, organizations, or nations on a collision course with us. The only solution for avoiding impending collisions is to change course. And the only long-term way to stay on a new course is for people to be satisfied that these behaviors will meet their needs and accomplish their goals.

Only love can chart courses for different people with different—often conflicting—needs. Fear and coercion can force people to change course, but it takes a huge expenditure of power and energy to maintain behavior by threat. Those holding power are in as much bondage and constriction as those who are oppressed and coerced. Only love frees both the powerful and the powerless to be all they were meant to be.

Many of us seem to think God's wish—and command—that we love everyone all of the time is castor oil. Isn't it amazing, though, when you think about it? Love is the most pleasurable activity in the universe. We pine for it. We treasure it. We love lovers, and we love ourselves when we're lovers.

So all God is asking of us is to participate in pleasure—and see what develops. God didn't say we had to change people or make them good. We don't have to be wise enough to solve everyone's problems. We are not responsible for others' actions toward us, what they do with our love, or how they interpret our care. We don't give up our life and joy or our good sense. We just get to love and care. To have our lives filled with the positive sense of moving with people rather than against them. To be a lover in the world. And at the end of the day to know that we pleased our God.

DISCUSSION QUESTIONS

1. What makes me mad? What signals is this giving me?

2. What helps me break anger chain reactions?

3. We've all received apologies that "worked" and some that didn't. What are characteristics of those apologies that truly mend relationships?

4. Are there apologies or restitutions I still need to offer?

7

Troublesome People

After spending most of my life in earshot of historic peace churches, I found their message had led me to be so hopeful about the power of God that I minimized human meanness and woundedness. Hearing down-to-earth Elise Boulding, sometimes called the mother of peace studies, say that "The world is filled with ornery people" helped me see this.

These ornery folks are in the workplace. Probably not a workplace in America lacks a troublesome person or two. We're all wounded. We've all found ways of coping that have rough edges. Some folks find their inner safety in the persona of the porcupine—then we're all pricked.

The very process of working brings out our best and worst. But this is no consolation to any of us hurt by the dysfunctions of co-workers, which play havoc with our work and poison our minds and spirits. We stew about the hurts when away from work. We seem stuck replaying the video in our minds. We plan and re-plan what we'll say. We try on costumes of anger, of piety, of sarcasm, of delicious revenge. Ultimately we avoid, escape, strike back, feel miserable.

We'd like to think that while these folks can make us feel bad, they have no real control over us. But they do. Mean people can hurt us, change the path of our career, ruin relationships. In extreme cases, they can literally take our lives. Sometimes we're delivered from their destruction; sometimes we pay full cost. Biblical and church history are filled with stories of those who paid full cost.

Troublesome People

What's this about? As long as God gives the gift of choice to every human being, there will be troublesome people. Every day, we reap the consequences of the wonder and glory of God *and* the consequences of generations of folks who have chosen against life and goodness. I suspect our lives aren't a prearranged road map issued at birth. Rather, we're on a journey, but many routes will get us there and will accomplish the will of God in the process.

When in college I didn't have access to a car. My church was across the city, and every Sunday generous people would make the trek to take me back and forth to services. The young man who usually picked me up turned the task into a game. He tried never to take the same route twice. I never knew what I'd see or encounter, but I knew that sooner or later we'd get to church. Our experience was a combination of our choice of path *and* the circumstances we encountered.

So it is with life. Ornery or good people can have a huge impact on our life's path. They can't change our destination—that's our choice. They can't ruin us as human beings—for how we meet and react to joy and tragedy is again our choice. And evil can't ultimately overcome good—that's God's choice.

But the shape of that process is a work in progress. Even Jesus didn't have to die. I know our theological shorthand says Jesus came to die. But God didn't make the religious establishment hate him. God didn't set up Pilate. We humans had a real choice. We could accept the great news of God in our midst—or we could continue in our brokenness and try to cast God out of our lives.

Jesus was certainly affected by choices and actions of broken, ornery people. But Jesus didn't stay wounded and dead. His death didn't even remain a tragedy. It became the vehicle by which the whole world has a chance to be saved. The worst became the best.

The good news is that we don't stay dead either. The very harm done to us becomes the vehicle of grace and redemption.

The work of God on the earth can't be stopped by human evil. The wonder of our being and the fruit of our obedience can't be conquered. Hard times are an occasion for the transformation of redemption among us.

Hard times also serve to make *us* more wonderful. I have a collection of cut crystal. I love the way it gleams and refracts the light. Some pieces are more beautiful and radiant than others. If one looks carefully at the difference, the most beautiful pieces are the ones that have the sharpest, deepest, most intricate cuts.

Look around. Those beautiful people of God radiant in our midst have sustained deep and sharp cuts. But they haven't been pulverized by pain and disappointment; they've become radiant and deeply empowered. I'd love to sail through life unscathed by trouble, but I know pain has its gift for me.

Jesus knew what he was talking about when he said, "Blessed are you when men revile you and persecute you and utter all kinds of evil against you falsely on my account. Rejoice and be glad. . . ."[1] Our culture likes to wallow in the morass of blame. Poverty made the teen violent. Being rejected as a child made the man mean. Being abused made the woman dysfunctional. Actually not. Pain brings us choice. We can choose to trust God in the pain—and it becomes gift to us. We can choose to mistrust and alienate ourselves from God in anger and blame—and it becomes tragic damage. The pain doesn't make us who we are. Our response to pain decides who we are.

We *are* capable of living triumphantly. We exhibit and celebrate that aspect of our humanness through participation in and appreciation of sports. Think about it. We think nothing of pushing ourselves and those we love to the limits of pain for conditioning and being "in shape." No pain, no gain. Parents and families willingly sacrifice time and money to put in the grueling hours of practice and preparation.

If the skill doesn't come easily, we don't give up. We look for coaches and mentors that help us be successful. We fail a zillion times, and we pick ourselves up and try again. We condition ourselves—physically and mentally—for the inevitable conflict on court or field. We're proud of taking hard hits. We don't blame and whine when injuries, winning, and losing change the textures of our lives. Tough stuff, difficult opposition, rookies who mess us up, coaches that hurt our feelings, game conditions that are uncomfortable—none deter us from the game. We thrive on it. We love it.

Yet when the same dynamics are present in the game of life, we seem unable to transfer the attitudes and skills. Christians are like a team that loves pep rallies, memorizing game plans, locker room camaraderie. We love the talk. We think the uniforms are cool. We love the commercial endorsements. But when we get on the field and take the first hit, have the pass intercepted, the kick blocked, we're shocked. We never really expected to play the game.

The workplace is the line of scrimmage. This is where the game is played. There are folks out there planning to block and tackle us. Rejoice. We're not sitting the bench; we're in the game. And it deserves every bit as much dedication, preparation, courage, enthusiasm, and teamwork as we humans can give it.

Troublesome people are part of the game of life. So how do we proceed?

Troublesome Situation or Person?

Whenever we hit a snag, we have to make a diagnosis. Is there a real and pertinent problem to be solved? If so, this is just a *troublesome situation*. The world of work is filled with problems to be solved. That's half the challenge and joy of work. A troublesome situation may be brought to your attention by someone you respect and admire. It may be discussed in a calm and engaging manner.

It may also be highlighted by her indignation, by his sullenness, or by a scathing memo. Remember, just because someone expresses herself unpleasantly doesn't mean she's troublesome. She may have had it up to here with a problem—or more likely, a series of problems. A troublesome situation just means there are still issues to be worked on. There needn't be a power struggle between you and those responding to the problem. You're all part of the solution. You're all on the same team. Feelings may need to be soothed. Misunderstandings may need to be talked through. Affirmation and friendship need to be given and taken. But this is the tug and pull of people working together in complex issues and processes. At the end of the day, you can look each other in the eye and be grateful for the other.

Troublesome people, on the other hand, aren't responding to a real and particular problem. You can recognize the troublesome person because his complaints often make little sense, she shows a pattern of troublesome behavior, and the result is that the person manipulates the situation. Troublesome people may *seem* to be presenting a problem. However, they're not looking for solutions. They're seeking to have their needs met. A mistake we often make when dealing with such people is to think solving the presenting problem will end the trouble. It doesn't, because the problem wasn't the issue but the person.

Troublesome people come in all sizes, shapes, genders, nationalities, strengths, and weaknesses. They range from mildly troublesome to totally disruptive. Sometimes their woundedness only emerges when a certain chord is struck. Others seem stuck in a mode of woundedness. The reasons for their pain are complex and varied. There is no one answer in working with troublesome people, but the call is always to love. That is one of the more difficult calls to answer.

Noticing

I often get ambushed by troublesome folk. I work, respond, and give and take as if we're on the same page. Then out of nowhere comes a response, a reaction, a behavior that surprises me. "Where did *that* come from?" I ask myself. Then it becomes clear the agenda has shifted. A personal agenda has been interjected into the task. Now I have two things to deal with—the task I thought we were all working on *and* the agendas of this person or group. My first response is irritation. I often feel self-righteous. "Why can't we just all get on with the business at hand?" I feel I'm being asked to take a detour to take care of someone's wounded feelings or misperceptions. I flinch from wasted time and futile effort. I don't want to hold someone's hand right now. I want to get the job done!

It takes effort to pull back from the momentum of the task. Often, since I enjoy my work, I'm having a wonderful time moving forward on a project. It not only feels like wasting time to leave the task; it feels like popping my balloon or raining on my parade. But the first task in dealing with troublesome people is to take notice. The behavior of a troublesome person is like that of a small child who keeps jostling the newspaper you're trying to read.

Troublesome people have well-practiced ways of manipulating you into noticing them. They may do it through saccharine sweetness that enrages or by acting out. But the bottom line is that you must take notice of them. Noticing may not be all they need; but it is always the beginning of what they want.

Many a problematic interaction can be avoided by noticing, *really noticing,* people. A few minutes checking in with one another about how we are and what's on our minds can save hours—or months—of labor later. Words of affirmation and trust at the beginning of a day, project, or meeting can diffuse many a time bomb. Such preventive measures keep us functioning well, even amid the wounds we all carry. They may provide the care mildly troublesome people need to be their best selves. Really noticing seriously troubled folks may not resolve their issues but will at least give us some awareness of their agenda so we won't be blindsided an hour later.

91

Compassion

Troublesome people bring out the worst in us. They know how to press our buttons. They know how to engage us so we have to attend to them. Sadly, troublesome persons are so wounded they would rather experience our anger than go unnoticed.

We struggle to find compassion for them. Their behavior almost automatically opens floodgates of anger, judgment, blaming, belittling. Their actions can be incompetent, irrational, inappropriate. They mess up well-laid plans. They generate unwelcome emotions.

Yet compassion is what's called for. Troublesome behavior is always a symptom of deep and persistent pain. If we were to know the internal terrain of these people and their lives, our hearts would break with compassion. We'd see how hurt, how courageous they are. We'd have no problem surrounding them with the love and tenderness of God.

But that's only half the problem. Not only are troublesome people deeply hurt; they're experts at covering that pain so no one can see or heal it. The troublesome folks you work with are miles past hoping something will fix their pain. They're firmly entrenched in behaviors they see as carving out a semblance of safety and self-respect. Somehow it's working for them. Probably not well—but enough to justify their persisting in such behaviors.

We are not their saviors. We probably weren't hired to be the company's mental health professional. However, we can be compassionately aware that such persons carry heavy backpacks through life.

Power

Power issues are foundational to much troublesome behavior. People learn their needs won't be met. They've also learned they feel safer if they have power. Power, in this context, is not the big stuff of finance and politics. Power is the subtle permission to do, to exert one's energy, to determine choices. We give and take power countless times a day.

Power is ability to effect an outcome. Suppose I want to take a walk in the middle of the work day. If I can get up and take that walk without reporting to anyone or experiencing repercussions, I have all the power in that situation. If I'm boss but have to tell my secretary and three other co-workers that I'm stepping out for a walk, I have some power but not all. My secretary may disapprove of my wasting time. Next week she may raise her eyebrows in a way that suggests suspicion of how hard I work. She may have no formal power over me, but she still has real power in the situation. Alternatively, I may be in a position that makes it unthinkable for me to take a walk unless I want to risk getting fired. In that situation I have virtually no power.

So we're all waltzing dances of power all the time. We have it, give it, share it, lack it. There is nothing sinister about power. Everyone must experience some power. Health and sanity demand it. Suicidal temptations come when we feel powerless. Remember the proverbial story about the boss who kicks the worker who kicks the wife who kicks the kid who kicks the cat? That's the chain of needing and taking power.

Most of us have learned to find power in functional ways—but troublesome people have not. They manipulate people and situations to gain a sense of power and control. And when folks are broken in heart and spirit, they don't care if they get that power positively or negatively. Their need eclipses care for others or awareness of consequences. We feel we're in a power struggle with troublesome people. And we are.

Now sometimes power can be shared. Doing so won't diminish us. However, it's not always possible to share power. There is power of being, personhood, spirituality, integrity that we can't share. There are workplace situations in which we hold total responsibility and must retain the power to fulfill it. We can't give power away because someone feels threatened; it's not always possible to give troubled people what they want.

Intercession

Chances are good that the troubled person who comes to mind is beyond simple remedies of noticing, caring, and appropriate power-sharing. The person feels like a steamroller in your life. Frankly, you don't want to deal with her. You just want him out of your life.

Christians aren't limited to the strategies of interpersonal psychology. God sees into the human heart. God loves the unlovable. God's spirit can penetrate the best-defended psyche. God wants us to intercede. Intercession is asking for help for another. We take this wounded brother or sister to our God who can heal and restore. We can't fix the pain of the person's life. But God can. We can't act wisely enough to help the person to health and trust. But God can. Intercession carries our paralyzed co-worker to Jesus.

Troublesome people are paralyzed by defense mechanisms. They can't break the cycle of their behaviors. So we tenderly take them to Jesus day after day in prayer and love. We try to see past the prickly spines of their attacks to the child that cries within. We deflect their irritable language upward as an SOS to God who saves. We release them into God's mercy and justice rather than keeping our own accounts—thus enacting forgiveness. This liberates our spirit from bondage to their extortions.

Prayer can be an act of words and language. It can also be an image. It can be visualizing a beam of warm light surrounding the person. It can be a picture of the person as a child being cuddled on a parent's lap. It can be an image of Jesus walking beside them. The Holy Spirit often gives us prayer pictures easy to hold amid demanding days. Prayer can be acts of love. Intentionally be kind to troublesome people. Think into their lives. Would those tickets to the ball game that you aren't getting to use give them unexpected pleasure? Do they love the fruit you just picked from your yard? Would they too enjoy the e-mail humor you just read? Include them in intentional acts of caring.

Teamwork

Use the systems in place

Solutions to many troublesome situations require teamwork. Businesses and organizations provide systems for checks and balances, accountability, appeals. Use such mechanisms. Use staff meetings, evaluation processes, comment boxes, ombudsmen, personnel offices, mediation services, and formal judicial protocols. As appropriate, prayerfully and caringly use mechanisms provided by your workplace.

Create systems in special instances

Unusual circumstances sometimes require creating teamwork where none exists. An intervention for a person with a drug or alcohol problem is an example of a group effort that works on behalf of friend or colleague. There are often more informal ways to work as a team on someone's behalf. Sometimes it's necessary for everyone to hold the line, say the "no." Sometimes we cooperate to encourage and affirm a discouraged co-worker. Sometimes we all share some of the work to lighten the load for someone who is struggling or has special needs.

When we organize, however informally, to help a co-worker, we risk embarrassing or demeaning the person. No one likes to be talked about in unflattering ways. No one wants to be the object of pity or disrespect. Everyone hates to be ganged up on! We need to be clear that any group effort flows from respect and care. There is no place for sarcastic humor, gossipy undertones, or sharing confidential information.

Have a spiritual fellowship

To be empowered at work we also need spiritual fellowship. I don't mean just going to church. I mean one or more persons who know what work is like for us. These are people we can tell about our work—our joys, difficulties—who will join us in prayer and caring.

We need such friends at two crucial points. First, we need people who will care for us. Troublesome people can damage us and our work. We need folks who bind us up, who help us find wisdom and ways forward. We need people to pray protection for us so our work is accomplished despite obstacles. We need to know we're not all alone in the workplace. We need folks with whom it's safe to rant and rave and let off steam. We need a place to complain and let our ouches air out.

Second, we need help with intercession. Prayer on behalf of others is magnified in effectiveness as persons of different perspectives and experiences pray from different angles.

I see this vividly in relationship with one of my best friends. She has a troublesome family member. Our prayers together are fuller and deeper than her prayers on her own would be. She is often so bruised in the relationship that she needs to rely on me for seeing the wounded inner child of the relative. She is often too close to the situation authentically to intercede. I'm removed from the pain and thus free to enter deeply into compassion for the relative. My friend needs me to carry that piece for her. She can't do it all. I'm there to help my friend; I'm also there to be a partner of intercession for her dear, pain-filled relative.

Sometimes it's hard to know if we're gossiping or praying. My rule of thumb is to double-check the motive and outcome of the sharing. If the aim of sharing is to diminish or harm, it's gossip. If the aim is to find wisdom so everyone is supported and empowered, then likely it's spiritual friendship.

When we send representatives to a missionary endeavor, we pray for them. Many groups make picture cards to put on the refrigerator so we remember to pray regularly for these ambassadors. We get newsletters that let us know problems encountered and God's miraculous works. In truth, most of us are on workplace mission assignment. We're doing the crucial work of bringing God's presence amid pain, sorrow, and brokenness. We're ambassadors of the Good News that God has come to live with us and transform all things.

We need teams that support each other in the workplace with the same spiritual attentiveness we give our missionaries. This is part of the work of the church. Millions of Christians depend on prayer or Bible study groups for such interdependence. Some have found groups of co-working Christians with whom to share. Others find support in their families. One arrangement doesn't fit all. But every worker needs a prayer partner or two. And the difficult work of being redemptive to a troublesome person needs a team of God's people.

What does God offer us amid troublesome people?

There are two sides to this question. Our side and the other person's side. What God's people can count on is that everything is useful. There is no promise that every project we have will magically be protected. There is no promise that the harm of troublesome people will not affect us.

There is a promise that *everything* is useful and goodness can't be vanquished. Actually there is humor in the situation. Picture an obstacle race—and imagine that every place the racer's feet touches something wonderful happens. So the cheating opponent arranges to have obstacle after obstacle put in the runner's path. This forces the runner to go here and there overcoming the obstacles. But not only does the runner indeed finish the race, but the runner's feet have touched many places and even more good has been done in the end.

Evil presents obstacles meant to discourage us and prevent our finishing the race, accomplishing the task, being God's radiant people on earth. But if we meet each obstacle simply with another outpouring of God's presence through us, then evil is befuddled. Goodness has multiplied in situations that would have been untouched.

Suppose you're driving along hoping for an uneventful trip. Things go "wrong." The more things go wrong, the more people you meet. You'd have passed through that town without stopping. In the end, you touch the mechanic, the waitress, the motel staff, and residents with the love of God.

This needn't mean you handed out tracts or quoted Scripture (though perhaps you did). It means you looked at each person with care and respect. It means that in each encounter you were expecting God to be present. It means that as you stayed connected to God, everyone you met was touched by Godness. As psychologist John Finch put it, "You are a sponge. Love is the water. Drink deeply at the ocean of Love so that you may be full, so that whoever touches you gets wet."[2]

The pitfall is disconnecting from God's love when things seem to go wrong. We stop seeing situations as opportunities. We often even fray our precious relationship with God by blaming God for not taking good enough care of us or not answering prayers. Then no good is done. Anger and irritation spew over everyone. And evil does get the last chuckle.

The consequences of troublesome people are that sometimes we have more obstacles to deal with. The good news is that through the love of God, increased good can be done.

The other side of the issue is the other person. We wish we could wave a healing wand over folks. But healing is a matter of cumulative choosings. God's goodness is never coercive, so we can't predict how others will respond. If we scan the human experience of loving the hard-to-love, we see a continuum of responses. Many times love shatters walls. Other times hearts harden and become intentionally cruel. Either case is a result of one more invitation of God's Spirit.

The Gospel of Mark shows us this dynamic. Two groups standing side by side in the presence of Jesus choose different responses. One praises and believes; the other sets out to kill Jesus. We haven't necessarily done something wrong because the "happy" ending eludes us. We can rest in knowledge that with each act of love, the Holy Spirit has one more opportunity to touch a life. That's a considerable gift. And it may be that the proverbial Chinese water torture of one drop of water after another may be effective for good as well as for evil.

I do know I can never predict who will respond to the love of God. No fail-safe outward indicator lets us know who is impervious to God's Spirit. Cruelty, insanity, hardened hearts are not necessarily indicators that a person is unreachable. "Niceness" and "moralness" are not necessarily indicators of openness. We simply sow the seed. Some will respond. Some will not. It's not our responsibility to control responses. Our responsibility is to sow good seed.

As my daughter walked out of the house to do another day's work with a troublesome person, she looked at me and said, "Well, perhaps this will be a good day. If it is, God will have really worked. And if it isn't, I'll know God is still working on it." She had it right.

DISCUSSION QUESTIONS

1. What at work brings out both the best and worst in us?

2. Does work accentuate my strengths or weaknesses?

3. Compare our capacity for hardship in athletics versus in spiritual endeavors. Why the difference?

4. Why is it hard to give troublesome folks what they need?

5. Are we supporting each other in our mission to the workplace? How could we do so more effectively?

8

Seductions

Needing control, feeling fear and anger, and working with troublesome people are big deals in our lives. But issues that pose even greater threats are more subtle. There are attitudes and routine behaviors that lead us into peril. But they're so normal, so culturally acceptable, so seemingly nourishing that we don't even see them.

For instance, we know pride goes before a fall. But in our proud moments nothing worries us—until we crash. Then we look back and trace the invisible footprints of prideful choices that led us to this unthinkable place.

We'd be deeply and eternally helped if we let the community of faith give us lifesaving feedback about subtle temptations when they're small and easy to change. But we don't. For most folks, this is private business. Heaven help the spouse or friend who dares call such behaviors to our attention.

I call root attitudes and behaviors that lead us astray *seductions*. They're seductions because they lead us so slyly away from the heart of God. We don't even notice the drift. They're seductions because they're the real tools of the Evil One. They're the invisible strings that keep us part of sinful culture. They're the silent chains that tow us out of God's power.

These are seductions of powers that are not of God. These are sirens of our culture that woo us away from the life of God. These are principalities and powers doing real battle with us.

Put on the whole armor of God, that you may be able to stand against the wiles of the devil. For we are not contending against flesh and blood, but against the principalities, against the powers, against the world rulers of this present darkness, against the spiritual hosts of wickedness in the heavenly places. Therefore take the whole armor of God, that you may be able to withstand in the evil day, and having done all, to stand.[1]

Contemporary illuminations of what we're up against come from Walter Wink's trilogy of the Powers.[2] Both the Apostle Paul and Walter Wink are wrapping language around a real but invisible reality. There are currents, winds, tornadoes of this invisible reality that constantly buffet us and sometimes sweep us up in horrific ways.

There is the invisible reality of God. There is the invisible reality of that which is not God. Both are real. Both have power and substance. Both become incarnate in the world around us. Wink points out that "every economic system, state apparatus and power elite *does* have an intrinsic spirituality, an inner essence, a collective culture or ethos. . . ."[3]

The world system has a spirit and a power. Thus our invitation to be God's people cannot ignore our real battles with the spirit of systems all around us. Perhaps we can grasp this concretely when we think of a mob scene. Here a group of normal, law-abiding people are caught up in a whirlwind. Some collective energy pulls them from ways of thinking and behaving. They become capable of participating in acts they'd usually consider unthinkable. In their behavior can be sensed the invisible phenomenon of which I am speaking.

To be sure, God is the highest power. Ultimately, all principalities and authorities will be reconciled through the cross.[4] It is our task to live out of the power of God amid wily and seductive counter forces. To do this, we must be aware. We need each other to alert us to the small print of our lives that needs examining and changing. Many a Christian has been sucked into the quicksand of the world system without having a clue that it's happening. On the surface, these seductions don't look contrary to the gospel message. That's why the power of their magnetic pull can blindside us.

There are significant workplace seductions.

Disrespect

This innocuous little seed germinates into great evil. When I reflect on the slippery slope that has led God's people into unethical business practices, immoral behavior, and disgracing the community of faith, it all starts with disrespect. Disrespect for boundaries, for rules and laws, for other people. Disrespect seduces us to become the center of our universe.

Disrespect is part of the spirit of our culture. Academic achievement often entails putting other persons and theories down. Scholarship too often means poking holes in other people's ideas. Business likes to picture itself in a fast track; this leads to inherent disrespect for what is measured, bounded, moderated. Those who make money harbor quiet disrespect for those who don't. Those with expertise think nothing of looking down on those who lack it. Winners needn't heed losers. In the currency of the world, disrespect elevates. It gives a temporary high. It's a glue that bonds people temporarily together; being disrespectful together is a cozy feeling.

However, disrespect makes us watch our backs for those who disrespect us. It isolates us from lifesaving feedback and accountability. It dismantles the barricades that protect us from falling off life's cliffs. It muffles the voice of God.

Christians are vulnerable to this spirit. We may begin by disrespecting those who don't believe or act as we do. We may accidentally inhale disrespect with our academic or athletic experiences. It may be a by-product of our "in" crowd. We may misread the blessings of God in our lives, forgetting our common condition. Disrespect may take root through a simple, unquestioning acceptance of the culture around us.

Respect is lifesaving. Respect isn't earned; it's a gift we give every person. It points to our acknowledgment of God's work in every life. It joins God in the steadfast love God has for all. Respect honors boundaries. Living on the edge is no kingdom virtue. Living in the middle of God's goodness and presence is the virtue. There is nothing edgy about that. We don't skirt and shade the truth. We don't cut corners. We don't flirt with loopholes. We don't live in the fast track. We plant our feet firmly in the Eternal Now—and we stand.

Depersonalizing

A companion seduction is to depersonalize. It's easy to cheat a company which seems a faceless monolith. "No one's getting hurt; it's just an insurance company." It's easy to be cruel to those in power when we refuse to acknowledge they're people like ourselves. Consumers forget how they'd like to be treated if on the other end of the phone or behind the desk or badge. Folks hurl words and trash at athletes who disappoint. Horror is heaped on national leaders day in and day out. Paparazzi hound celebrities. Good people do such things because they make folks objects rather than persons.

Horrors are enacted in the workplace because we dehumanize. The bottom line can become our god only when we mass Jack, Mary, Mario, Rita, and Hobart into a lump called "workers." We can only live out our chilling prejudices when we see politicians, rich folks, poor folks, managers, and welfare mothers as objects to be treated as we wish. Exploitation can't happen if we take each other's lives into account.

God's people must share God's heart. God doesn't toss away people as objects or generalizations. God's heart stays tuned to every person's anxieties; every tear is tenderly acknowledged.[5] God's not looking for the least God can give people. God lavishes abundance on us.

Look at nature. Creation's not a stripped-down model. God could have given us justice; instead we're offered mercy.

God could have provided subsistence; instead we're wondrously provided for. God could treat us like things, but God elevated us to co-heirs with Jesus.

The seductions of the world lure us from God's phenomenal love. They cheapen life to the level of objects and stuff. It requires little effort to be the only person in our universe. Everyone else is a prop, role, or function. If disrespect appeals to our desire for status and power, depersonalizing appeals to our laziness. Taking people into account is hard, endless, messy, and costly work. So we slip into an easier way—and have a hard time even noticing the harm we do.

Infidelity

Infidelity is failure to be faithful to a commitment. Although we usually associate the word with unfaithfulness to a spouse, a spirit of infidelity also lures us. Our lives are filled with commitments. Some are so natural we don't even think about them.

For instance, when we get a driver's license we're making a commitment to the community to drive according to the rules. Our commitments to drive on the correct side of the road, to stop at red lights, to yield the right-of-way are essential for any of us to travel safely. Most of us understand the wisdom of fidelity in the driving process.

Unfortunately, in our society there are few other commitments we take so seriously. Feelings have superseded commitments; impulse has become a virtue. "Just do it." The fabric of a culture depends on hundreds of fidelities. The cloth of the kingdom of God is based on fidelity to relationships. Fidelity to the God who loves us. Fidelity to all other humans. Fidelity to the environment. Fidelity to our truest self. Fidelity to our own explicit and implicit commitments.

The proof of the pudding that we're God's people most often comes as folks observe how faithful we are to our commitments. Yet more harm has been done to the cause of Christ by the infidelities of Christians than by our apostasies and heresies. We break trust in business practices; we break trust with our promises. We break trust in our attitudes and in our relationships. We break trust in our marriages and in our parenting. We break trust in our communities.

Our lives are filled with thousands of commitments. When we choose a residence, we're committing to being a neighbor. We make financial commitments to pay mortgage or rent, maintenance, taxes. But we also have implied commitments to be considerate in handling noise and the impact of our lives on those around us. We make a commitment to care and be available in crisis. A person of God is responsible to think into *all* commitments of being a neighbor—and making sure God is glorified in every facet of fidelity.

We associate fidelity with sexual faithfulness. That is a critical mark of the person of God. But the marriage relationship also includes fidelity of time and energy to sustain long-term relationships. It includes fidelity to life so sexual expression is prepared to welcome the life that may be created. Fidelity to the possibility of new life entrusted to us *precedes* acts of sexual expression and love.

In a world of competing fidelities, we must prioritize. We must say some "no's." We can't promise everything to everyone. There must be boundaries to our commitments. That's the only way to be faithful people. So we don't promise to have dinner sometime when we know we'll have a hard time being faithful to the offer. We don't promise our child something, then forget about it. We don't say we'll have the report on the desk by tomorrow morning if we can't deliver. We think about what we say and do. We say only what we can mean. Our yes is yes. Our no is no.[6]

On a grander scale, we have competing fidelities between home, work, community of faith, friends, family. We sometimes feel pulled by horses running in opposite directions. We've been falsely led to think we can have it all. If we're going to be people of fidelity who honor God, we must make choices. If we're going to commit our lives totally to work, then we shouldn't commit to marriage and family.

Conversely, if we're called to the commitments of relationships, then work will have to be measured and bounded. There are many ways to arrange our lives in obedience—but whatever that is for each of us needs to be a thoughtful choice allowing us to keep fidelity in every aspect of life.

Work is based on mutual commitments. Some are written, like a contract, an invoice, a loan. Others, like loyalty, are assumed. Fidelity in the workplace is often apparent in the details. Being present to the workplace for the entire workday. Accomplishing the tasks entrusted us. Giving and taking face to face, rather than behind the back. Keeping faith with salaries, benefits, and raises. Giving credit where due. Abiding by rules of the trade in relationships with the competition. Telling the truth. Treating each person with respect and dignity.

Companies have corporate commitments. There is a commitment to the fidelity of product or service. There is an implicit promise to do and be what is advertised. There are commitments to the welfare of employees, communities, the environment. There are commitments to participate lawfully in an economic system. These are non-negotiables for Christ's people.

Actually the whole world knows what Christianity is supposed to stand for. We're supposed to be the people who love and are merciful and can go the distance. When we break trust with our beliefs and slip down to the common denominator of the world around us, everyone takes notice. They rightfully expect us to be nonconformed to this world. We're called to a higher accountability. We're light and salt. If we lose our savor, what good *are* we?[7] If business as usual dominates our lives, the world's in trouble.

DISCUSSION QUESTIONS

1. Seductions are mirages that betray us. What do disrespect, depersonalization, and infidelity *seem* to offer? Why are they so tempting?

2. How does our faith sometimes breed disrespect?

3. Who are the persons in our lives that are easy to depersonalize? How do we treat them differently than folks we know personally?

4. What are commonplace situations in which we can be more faithful to our commitments?

5. How can we help one another resist the seductions of the culture around us? How have people successfully helped us? How have people had good intentions but been unhelpful?

Part Three

POWER
OF
PRESENCE

Sacraments for the Workplace

The world would be brought to Me so soon, so soon,
if only all who acknowledge Me as Lord, as Christ,
gave themselves unreservedly to be used by Me.
I could use each human body as mightily
as I used My own human body
as a channel for Divine Love and Power. —God Calling

A sacrament is a visible expression of the invisible God. A sacramental moment is a sacred time in which God's presence is real to us, touches us, blesses us. The gossamer curtain that often hides the face of God is pulled aside. We see, feel, know God. The church has institutionalized sacramental moments. In many church traditions, we're accustomed to thinking of sacraments in that context. But in reality we're living sacraments. Our lives are the occasions when God is visible to those around us. There are distinct times when who we are, what we do, and what we say convey God's blessing. These are the most powerful witnesses God's people can make.

Work is occasion for many sacramental moments. We're enriched when we open our eyes to the incredible opportunities for ministry and witness that daily lie at our fingertips.

Gratefulness

Gratefulness and praise are like a speed dial to heaven. Gratitude is the quickest way to make a connection with God.

God is so worthy of praise. We're immersed in the goodness of God's love. We're never wrong when we speak of this, or naïve when we look back at the face of God and beam with grateful love.

By the same token, a grateful spirit is an opening for others to perceive God. Two incidents from my own experience illustrate. One turning point of my spiritual life happened in the context of such joy.

I was working at the church office when our pastor, Oscar, came bounding into the office. His face was aglow. He was grinning from ear to ear. His body language was alive and vibrant. "What happened to you?" I exclaimed.

"Oh, I just had the most wonderful time with Jesus! He was in the seat next to me coming across town—and we had the most wonderful conversation," Oscar responded. Off he loped into his office to meet his next appointment.

My world spun around. I had been a faithful Christian all my life but had never really thought about having a good time with Jesus. Now I loved to think of it. Of course we could be having a good time with Jesus!

My sense of God's presence enlarged in significant and lasting ways. Oscar gave me a sacrament of joy and gratefulness. God moved into my life with a wonderful and powerful life-changing moment.

Some time later, I discovered that my own grateful spirit was having the same effect. I have a habit of including Jesus in my verbal conversations. If Jesus is really with us all the time, I have a lot of things I want to talk over. And I see no reason not to include Jesus in the conversation when we're together. As I learned from Oscar, Jesus became a real person present in every interaction.

So one day I was driving with a friend. The day was incredibly beautiful. As we were soaking in the joy of the world around us, I addressed a sentence to God. "God, you really did good when you made this. It's terrific. Love it."

Sacraments for the Workplace

Inasmuch as talking to God in the middle of conversation was no big deal to me, I thought nothing of the comment. But later I found out that the spiritual turning point for my friend was that moment of grateful conversation with God. The simple act of verbal appreciation had been sacramental—and through it God marvelously met her condition.

Being grateful is like opening a nesting egg. One gratefulness leads to another. I'm grateful for my washing machine. On a daily basis, I give thanks for that convenience. I feel the blessings of those who have served me through designing, creating, selling, delivering, and maintaining it for me. I can see the faces of the persons who helped me choose the best model for my needs, the men who delivered it with care to my home. I don't know the folks who thought of a better design, created a more efficient cycle, who manufactured all the component parts, who assembled each piece on a factory line. But their integrity and faithfulness to their work blesses me daily.

Such gratefulness has a way of connecting us to joy. It feels terrific to reach out through time and space and thank all those folks I've never met but who have blessed me. It's easy to sense the interconnected love of God running through our lives.

Then I realize there's more!—all the persons who make it possible to have the water and electricity to power the machine. Those who dedicated their lives to learning and applying the laws of physics to make it possible. There is God who stands behind creation so willing to share the secrets of the creator's mind. A simple grateful glance at the washing machine is a powerful path to the heart of God. It takes us directly to loving God and loving our neighbors.

Gratefulness is an underused attitude. We're amazingly grumpy people. We're flooded with gracious provisions. We receive the service and faithfulness of millions of folks. We're graced with a beautiful country. For every ornery and troublesome person there are scores of individuals who offer their gifts without fanfare or credit. We reap the goodness of their lives moment by moment.

Go to work tomorrow morning and look at all the things you have to be grateful for. Let your eye fall on any object. Begin to trace its creation in the spirit of praise. Feel the connection to all who have make this object available to you. And if someone has erred, think how faithfulness of others outweighs this error. In the balance of things, gratefulness will always prevail if we have eyes to see.

The world is alive with things and people worthy of praise. Yet the real transforming power of God's people comes when we take the next step of giving thanks for these gifts. Thankfulness is like a beam of light connecting God to the human experience. Whenever we enact gratefulness, God's power is liberated into that situation. This is the key to transforming all things.

When we grasp this reality, we begin the adventure of giving thanks for things that don't appear praiseworthy. Most of us usually start our toddling praise with things that we can squint at to figure out how they might be transformed. We need to tread carefully here because the risk of cheapening another's pain is high. But if we squint just right we can sense how the birth of a handicapped child is a gift. We gain clues to how deeply that particular gift of suffering can bless the world.

If we've lived life long enough, we've sensed that disappointments also can be protections. I learned this dramatically while a child. My aunt and uncle were great world travelers. They were particularly excited about the voyage they were to take on the *Andrea Doria*. But they missed the departure. They were bitterly angry and disappointed. Yet within days their anger melted into gratefulness. This was the voyage on which the *Andrea Doria* sank. What appeared disaster was blessing in disguise.

Our lives are crammed with blessings in disguise if we're God's people! Everything is working together for the deep desires of our hearts. So step out; affirm this. Don't always be amazed after the fact. Give God credit here. We waste precious hours grumbling and complaining when the very things we're grumbling about are giving us gifts. We're like the child who, on Christmas morning, grumbles because the presents are wrapped rather than in plain sight. I know life doesn't tie things up with pretty bows. But God does promise that even if it is meant for evil, God means it for good.[1]

The adventure heightens. Look around at work. What things frustrate you? Who are the people that make life difficult? The troubles may be mundane or large. Take that chair killing your back. Or that life-threatening disease. Take someone whose style irritates you. Or an eruption of deep evil. Whether petty or huge, focus the laser of God's power on those things, those people by thanking God for them. Thank God for their presence in your life. Thank God for the work to be done through and with them. Thank God for the wonderful ways you're going to weave this into the pattern of your life. You're an inspirational story in the making!

I carry an image that helps me with this process. The traditional way to make an oriental rug is for several villagers to work on the design together. I'm told that when they make a mistake they don't rip out their work. Rather they incorporate the mistake into the design—and the rug only increases in beauty. God is weaving our lives with us. And all things are woven into the beauty of our being.

Thanksgiving is liberating and exciting. However, there is one more level of empowerment. There is true sacrifice of praise.[2] Evil is vanquished through the sacrament of praise. There are things so horrible we can't see through them to the silver lining. Our hearts can't comprehend any transformation. These are times we focus the laser of thanksgiving against all our senses and better judgment.

How can you thank God for the death of a child? The horrible strife in Bosnia or Rwanda? Divorce? Cancer? Hitler?

Those who died on the *Andrea Doria*? How can we hold the oppressions of the economic system in gratefulness? How can we be thankful for the hatchet man who pares the company to the bone, who exploits the remaining workers for a corporate profit for stockholders? How can we be grateful for the boss who makes our days a living hell? How can we be thankful for the stress taking our health from us?

Merlin Carothers discovered the power of praise in his ministry. What God taught him was that when we offer the boggling sacrifice of praise at the very point of horror and evil, it again liberates the power of God to change things. His books and his ministry chronicle miracle after miracle that befell folks who obediently thanked God in all things.[3]

If we're willing to follow Jesus the second half of the journey into the sacrifice of praise, nothing can stand against the power of God. Life can throw its worst at us and only more good will result.

Take a Bozo clown balloon with weighted bottom. You can knock it down. All the way down. But it can't stay down. Likewise, you can knock down grateful people. You can even kill them. But they won't stay dead. Their spiritual legacy will keep on reaping goodness infinitely. More and more good will be done. The only way to stop the work of God is to stop a grateful spirit.[4]

So let gratefulness be the prevailing breeze in your soul. Let it spill from your tongue, your smiles, your memos. Let it infuse your creations. Let it oil your interactions.

As simple as it is, this is one of the most powerful witnesses to the Gospel of Jesus Christ in the universe. A grateful spirit is the key to changing the world. It's a sacrament of God's transforming presence among us.[5]

Forgiveness

My friend Joyce called. Her son, Jeremy, had been in an automobile accident with his baby-sitter. As I rushed across town to be with her, my heart was filled with prayer, of course. The wonderful news was that while everyone was shaken up, no one was injured. With grateful hearts we continued the prayer together, asking God that Jeremy not carry fears about cars, the baby-sitter, or leaving parents. To our delight, those prayers were answered. The next day Jeremy jumped unhesitatingly into the car with the baby-sitter.

A few days later we were having afternoon coffee when the phone rang. Soon Joyce came with her hand over the phone. "Jan, this is the insurance company wanting to give us a settlement for psychological pain and suffering to Jeremy. I can't take money for something God already fixed, can I?"

We thought for a moment, then agreed in unison, "No, you can't make someone pay for damages that don't exist."

So she declined the settlement. It was a gutsy thing to do because their finances could have used an infusion of unexpected cash. But she was right: we can't have it both ways.

Forgiveness seems a similar issue. God brings good from whatever life throws at us. So we can't turn around and extract a pound of flesh from those who harm us. Forgiveness is releasing, just as Joyce released both baby-sitter and insurance company from owing her anything. Forgiveness is the sacrament that acknowledges God's transforming work in our midst even when we don't see or understand it.

Forgiveness is also the sacrament that acknowledges who is God. God has reserved the right to be judge, to keep people accountable, to take vengeance. Vengeance isn't ours to impose. Forgiving one who harms us is a tangible way we demonstrate our relationship with God. If we're god of our lives, then of course we must blame, punish, extract apologies and restitution.

There has to be accountability. The issue isn't whether or not to have it but whose job description it's in. Enforcing justice isn't part of *our* job description. Our job is to forgive and release. God's job is to deal with the harm. No one finally gets away with anything. God keeps track of judgments to be made.[6]

Forgiveness is a well-kept mental health secret. Forgiveness, like praise, puts us in right position with God and the world. And it heals us.[7] We don't forgive as a favor to the transgressor. We forgive to be kind to ourselves.

Forgiveness opens all channels to flow with God's love and power because it aligns us with how God is. God forgives. If we're like God, we forgive too. That's the mind of Christ. Not to forgive closes channels and severs us from God.

Jesus tells us forgiveness is only common sense. God has forgiven all of us so much. We walk clean and clear because of the generosity of our Lord. So it's illogical to turn around and be cruel to those who need our forgiveness. Forgiveness has no preconditions. It doesn't depend on the severity of the crime. It doesn't depend on the other person at all. Forgiveness is about us. It's a mark of what kind of person we are. It's the mark of who we serve.

Forgiveness keeps us healthy. If we had a psychological x-ray, we could see that every unforgiven hurt is like Velcro waving in the current of life. It affixes to every similar pain that floats by. The original injury becomes a magnet for more and more of the same. The tragedy is that a person has been truly injured. But if forgiveness doesn't heal the wound, it remains a sore that keeps being re-infected. And time doesn't heal it but only allows for collecting more and more hurt.

The only way to draw a line in the sand, to say "enough is enough," is to forgive. Forgiveness takes the Velcro off. Pain can come but doesn't keep piling up anymore. The wound heals. Our bodies are free to flow with health. Our minds are liberated from obsessions with painful situations.

Forgiving is a simple act of releasing. Release the person into the hand of Jesus. Release results of the sin into God's transforming power. Release yourself into the love of God to be healed, restored, vindicated.

Do this as many times as you need. Grudges and revenge become habits. They don't always go away with one act of release. Each time the injustice grabs you and you feel the anger rising, again let it go. It's too destructive to retain. Open your hands; drop it. Holding someone in unforgiveness is like trying to hold a white hot coal: it will only burn your hand.

You know you're clear when you find yourself not needing the person to make it up to you. The event may eventually fade from memory, but more likely it will simply take its place as a fact of your past with no emotional baggage still attached. The goal is not to fuss over hurts. Release and walk on.

Sometimes unforgivenesses is anchored deep in our psyches and pasts. There are several ways to proceed when injuries weave back through our life, when we settle one matter and another pops into consciousness. Not to worry. One path forward is simply to take each wound in stride. We remember it. Let it be what it was. Let the pain and hurt rise in our being. We don't have to stuff it down or make excuses anymore. We now have tools to handle it that we didn't have then. Now we can release the person who sinned against us. We can release ourself to God's tender care able to go backward and forward in time. We can release consequences we've had to bear in intervening months or years. Let healing flow back into that memory.

Another way to accomplish healing is to go to the root pain, if known. When we release the originating pain, all the pains attached to it tend to float harmlessly away.

One sentence caused a friend of mine excruciating pain when he was a young boy. His uncle looked at him in anger and exclaimed, "You're never going to amount to anything!"

That sentence seared my friend's heart. For years he saw and heard every comment, every situation through the lens of the script that he'd never amount to anything. A successful life and professional accomplishment couldn't erase the pain. He could tolerate no criticism because it signified he was worthless. No affirmation could fill the abyss of his self doubts. Thus pain heaped upon pain.

There will be no end to pain until this wounded friend looks back on the memory of that uncle, looks him in the eye, and forgives him. Then he will begin to find freedom as years of ensuing hurts are unlocked.

The virtues of forgiveness in the workplace can't be overstated. When work hurts us, staying in the flow of forgiveness is the best gift we can give ourselves. Forgiveness keeps us connected to God so something unexpectedly wonderful can happen. It keeps us healthy, so we can be everything we were meant to be. It keeps interactions clear so we don't have to play games. When we forgive, heaven and earth are one.

Prayer

Prayer is another way we focus the power and love of God on a specific circumstance. Scripture tells us to pray without ceasing.[8] We understand intuitively that this means prayer is more than words. There are hundreds of wonderful books on prayer.[9] Experiencing the power of prayer in the workplace is a marvelous adventure. Here are ways to keep the lines of prayer constantly open during the workday.

Prayers of words

We're accustomed to prayers having words. Whether we speak or think them, much of our praying happens through language. We converse with God. This Divine conversation is as varied and diverse as any human conversation. We talk about ourselves. We talk about others. We dialogue. We think out loud together. We ask for help and for things. We ask questions for reasons of information, curiosity, affection. We express ourselves and our feelings. We compliment and affirm others. We murmur affections and responses. Language is the window into our souls.

Sharing language with God is our most natural way of being with God. God is here and we talk. It's natural to include God in the conversation about work. We enjoy, complain, seek help, work together. Work is important to us; we have much to talk with God about in it.

There are jobs in which the inner conversation of language never has to stop. That's part of the joy of menial or repetitive labor. The mind is free to be present with God while the tasks are performed. Great ministries of prayer and praise can be carried forth while pushing a broom or pruning a bush.

Of course other labors require intense mental concentration. The inner and outer conversations of life have to cease. Yet prayer can go on.

Prayer without words

The link between God and ourselves can be through images as well as words. So a picture in your mind can constitute a full and powerful prayer. You can have a detailed conversation with God about problems with your co-worker. You can also simply picture God taking your co-worker's hand. Each time you return to the picture, the prayer is being prayed. Amazing miracles have come simply from holding an image in heart and mind.

One of my image prayers is Light. Light is an attribute of God, so I picture all kinds of light. Beams. Sunlight. Lamplight. Floodlights. Flashlights. Sunlamps. Lasers. Light is versatile. There is a light image for any situation. I can pray an image of light into a situation as easily as I can flip a light switch. This leaves my mind free for focus on work, yet the prayer goes on.

Many people love the prayer of music. Tunes can flow through us while we're immersed in other tasks. Prayer and worship is often continuous when we carry music inside.

There are infinite, creative ways we and God can discover the language of our relationship that flows unbroken through the workday. There is no one correct way. Prayers without words are as unique and special as any of us. They're well worth the experimentation it takes to find and practice them. They're the sustaining power that keeps us safe and loved in the thick of the action, wherever we are. They're the constant hand of God's presence on our back that lets us know we're never out there alone. They're the worldwide web connecting us to the source of all wisdom.

Prayers for ourselves

We're familiar with the frantic prayers for help we throw out to God during the day. We know the sweet comfort and well-being of working in the centeredness of God's presence. We probably know how to seek God's help as partner in the labor. We can expand this constancy of companionship with wordless prayers. If we know our inner adolescent becomes competitive and defensive, then we can have an inner image of God as parent smiling at us throughout the day. If we find ourselves suddenly feeling little and not professional, we can see ourselves safe in Jesus' lap. If we feel beleaguered and alone, we sense Jesus by our side. If we've made a mistake and feel shame creeping up the back of our neck, we can see God making something of our mess.

Prayers for others

Prayer is a gift we can give those around us. There are prayers of blessings. One of the endearing habits of Mother Teresa was blessing people she encountered. Walk into a room and simply bless each person in your mind. Bless folks in rush hour traffic. Bless customers. Bless products you make. Bless the people you work with. Bless all people you see during a day. A blessing is a gift of God's Presence. It's a divine kiss on the forehead. There may be occasions in which formal, verbal blessings are in order. This may be especially true in organizations trying to be intentionally Christian. Occasions of blessing one another are affirming and empowering.[10]

Sacraments for the Workplace

Work is an interdependent process. Everyone counts in the workplace. Thus it stands to reason that praying for others to be and do their best too is important! We don't have to walk around with an altruistic halo to know that work goes better when all function at their best. Through prayer we can help. Much of God's power for the workplace is overlooked because we have failed to understand the merit of praying for others.

This is illustrated by two incidents of union/management mediation. The first situation involved our friend, Don, labor negotiator for a large West Coast company. He was involved in a particularly difficult negotiation. It appeared no headway was being made. He was finding it hard to communicate meaningfully with the union negotiator.

The night before the strike was to start, Don asked for wisdom from our prayer group. The only sense we had was that he was to go into that crisis situation the next day and focus on loving the other negotiator.

So he did. The negotiator ranted, raved, and ranted some more. Don just kept loving him. Finally the negotiator's voice trailed off. The crisis was averted in a way no one could understand. The power of love had solved the unsolvable.

Several years later I was telling this story in a sermon to illustrate the power of love to solve practical problems. After the service, a man warmly shook my hand. "I wish I had met you twenty years ago," he said. He told me that he had just retired as a management negotiator for a major company in his area. As I spoke he had become angry. He had been a Christian his whole life. He had always prayed over every negotiation in which he'd been involved. Yet he'd never had such a miracle in his career. As I was speaking, he asked God why.

God gave him this answer: "You were always praying for yourself. I asked you to pray for the others."

I suspect we've only tapped the tip of the prayer iceberg because we underestimate how important it is to pray for those opposing us or blocking our way.

Prayers of alignment

We need to pray for ourselves and others. That's a natural part of our relationship with God. However, the entrance into making a difference in the world comes when the prayers align our heart with God's. These prayers are more listening than talking. They seek the specific will of God for that day.

We know what God's general purpose for us is—to love others. But of all the people who cross your path today, which ones does the Spirit draw your attention to? What act of love is your mandate and privilege this afternoon? Answers to such prayers require opening our senses to the whispers of God.

Prayers of alignment are also action prayers. They're an active pursuit to hear and to do. Indeed we may need divine conversation to discover why it's so hard to see the world through God's eyes. Part of the prayer may be our laying down our notions and feelings to join God. If God loves the street person, then we love the street person and discern how to express that. If God loves the competition, then we learn to exhibit our own care and respect for the competition.

This is what the gospel is all about. Being like Christ. Translating and demonstrating the heart of God in every arena of our lives. This is how the world is being redeemed. Everything in our spiritual life up to this point is preparation. *This* is what we were meant to be.[11]

Servant's Heart

Jesus, Son of God, entered human experience with a servant's heart. The road to greatness lies through servanthood.[12] Many a pitfall in the workplace can be avoided by maintaining a servant's heart toward task and people. There is no position that does not serve. Even the United States president is to serve the people.

The workday is a minefield. Scores of issues can blow us out of the water. We may need people to respect us. We may need to be right. We may need everything to be fair. We may be seeking love. We may need to control. We may be looking for a safe cocoon. We may need always to keep all our options open so we feel free. We may need an organization we can believe in and belong to, one that won't let us down. We may need to know more and have more information. No matter what we need, the workplace will let us down. People *will* push our buttons. The only way not to get tangled in angers and disappointments is to approach our work with a servant's heart.

Jesus redefined servanthood. He led us there as the only space of freedom. In being servants of the world, we become friends of God. In focusing on generous-hearted service, we find our needs met. In offering up our work, our wisdom, and our talents in service, we find surprising happiness.

Here is the divine paradox that saves Christians from the world's woes. We're like mountain streams. We rise from a spring of living water. We tumble downhill because that's our nature. We flow over, through, and around the landscape with unconscious abandon and charm. We're not diminished if folks drink from us. We're not insulted if they don't. If some eager beaver dams us up, we become the refreshing pool—perhaps deep and still enough for children to swim and dive in with joy. We seem insignificant; we often don't even have a name. Yet we're the vital link in the waters that give life to the earth.

DISCUSSION QUESTIONS

1. Why do gratefulness and forgiveness seem so difficult? What are benefits of complaining and holding people in unforgiveness?

2. When did something seem to go wrong but turn out to be for the best?

3. What situations make us feel justified for not forgiving?

4. What nonverbal prayers are helpful during our workday?

5. In what areas of life do we find it easy to remain aligned with God's viewpoint? Where is it hard?

6. How can we have a servant's heart without feeling like a doormat or a worthless person?

10

Faith in the Public Arena

We live in a paradox. We take pride in having religious freedom. It's true we have the privilege of gathering for worship. But when we try to live our faith, we find we're not so free after all. We're timid about letting our light shine at work. It may help to examine what we face as we translate faith into living, working action.

Unspoken Rules

Cultures are strange birds. Our North American culture is as strange as any other. The last few decades have seen an upheaval in the divisions between private and public. Not so long ago a woman's ankle or a man's chest were private, not to be seen. You might have discussed religion over dinner but never sex. Virtues were public; sins were private. In these two cases, as in others, values are now inverted. Sex is a public matter, but spirituality is embarrassingly private. Sins are no big deal, but virtues are secrets.

I've spoken in churches across the country. Often they've been small congregations struggling to keep a worshipping community together. Nothing special on the outside. And seemingly little special on the inside. Services tended toward dull. Families came year after year due to habit. Yet, when I probed, I usually discovered these folks had *well-kept secrets*. The secrets weren't sins. All knew each other's sins.

The secrets were the works of God! A healing here. A marriage saved there. A miraculous deliverance from danger. God was alive and well, but even close friends and relatives didn't know each other's stories. They were locked in the room of life marked "PRIVATE." As I struggled to understand why these wonderful testimonies to the good news had been tucked in total privacy, folks shrugged their shoulders and said things like these:

"I didn't want someone to think I was holier than thou."

"My mother told me to not have a big head."

"I don't know. I never thought about it."

Communities around them were in pain over tragic illnesses, broken families, dangers of daily life. And here were people who had faced these things and learned the power of God. But they weren't talking. They didn't mean to be cruel, but in a sense they were—as if they had a secret antibiotic and were refusing to share it. The upside-down, backward values of our culture had these fine people thinking they were virtuous for keeping God a secret even as they actually withheld tremendous good news.

The unspoken workplace rules are similar. Everything is fair game for conversation—except our inner reality, our vibrant relationship with God. We don't mention ongoing conversations with Jesus. We don't give credit to prayers we've been offering day in and day out. Few know about the give and take, the failings and successes. They're locked away. Private. Keep Out.

Authenticity means showing outside what's real inside. If we're having a vibrant relationship with God, there are natural ways and times this should show. We don't have to make special efforts to "witness." Our vitality flows naturally if we simply tell the truth. In my office, it's known that I talk to God about everything. My co-workers know I seek wisdom when facing tough problems. They know where the great idea came from when I bound into their office with a solution. I don't have to do anything but be me. That's part of who I am. If I feel like putting words to it, I'm free to do so. If I don't feel like verbalizing my interactions with God, I don't have to. Once I—and you—have taken our relationship with Jesus out of the closet, we have freedom to do what feels right at the moment.

We feel the pressure of unspoken rules. We were enculturated into them, but no one is standing guard to punish us. We've become our own inner police. So the struggle to let our spiritual life show is one inside our minds and emotions. No one will hurt us if we mention what Jesus and we talked about over breakfast. Our hyperventilation stems from deep inner conditioning. The only way to overcome our hidden fears and messages is to step out of that proverbial closet.

Everyone's conditioning is different. Though I was enculturated into a Christian home and church, folks didn't say the word *Jesus* in regular conversation. They said "Lord" or "God" or maybe "Christ Jesus"—but not Jesus. That puzzled me because I thought Jesus was our best friend. I couldn't figure out why everyone seemed so embarrassed to say his name. So I decided since Jesus was my real friend, I'd talk out loud to Jesus anytime. That was one of the wiser decisions I've made. It broke the invisible barrier that keeps our real life with God hidden from the world. It made Jesus the natural part of my life he is. This habit has made authenticity come more easily for me. And because Jesus loves folks, people around me are delighted to have Jesus in my life. It's a good deal for them.

Witnessing is being transparent about ourselves. It's not pressuring someone else into thinking or doing anything. It's simply the gift of letting people know what's real for us. There is nothing embarrassing about that; this is normal and appropriate in the workplace.

Love Dictates Sharing

Sharing is a process in which each person chooses to participate. Much of the horror of religious witnessing has come from foisting unsolicited and unshared information. The typical image of witnessing is having someone cram something down your throat! This isn't witnessing. It isn't what Jesus did, or what Peter, Paul, or John offered. People *gathered* to listen to Jesus. They came from miles around to hear him. The disciples engaged kings and beggars in witness when there was occasion for it.

Even the great street sermons were in response to crowds gathered to hear. On the day of Pentecost, the multitudes came and asked what was going on. This was the prelude to Peter's great sermon that brought 3,000 converts.[1] Stephen's sermon was a response to being seized and brought before the council.[2] Paul's famous sermon in Athens was a response to his being forcibly "invited" to present his new teachings.[3] Wherever we got the idea that witnessing is talking *at* folks, it wasn't from the New Testament. As the good news is about relationship, not dogma, so witnessing is about dialogue, not monologue.

How and where we share depends on circumstances and the shared situation. Love can tell when and when not to put words to internal realities. People ask for our opinions, our insights, our processes when ready for them. If we've been faithful in the living, the sharing will come out of invitation. The Holy Spirit is working in the hearts of all people all the time. It's not our job to compose the Holy Symphony directing how everyone should believe and act. Our job is to play our part when the Divine Conductor points the baton at us.

If we do take an initiative and offer our faith unsolicited, we do so out of deep love and tender concern, never a spirit of condemnation. We must truly be "for" the person.

Our Life as Witness

Our faith is always visible whether we like it or not. Who we are constantly shows. If our life is being lived as a continual sacrament, if we're the living sacrifices of Romans 12—then

God is liberated to be active wherever we are, whether in thought or physical presence. If we do our job with a grateful and forgiving spirit, we're witnesses to our Lord. If we're competent and live a centered, joyful life, the workplace takes notice. If we can be counted on to lend the helping hand, to walk with our struggling colleagues, to use every ounce of our achievement in service of others, we give glory to God. If we face adversity, injustice, and hardship with praise and humility, we overcome all evil. We can say God words all we want, but our lives are the bottom line. For better or worse, we're the reflection of God in our workplace. Do we do God justice?

Limitations in the Workplace

There are rules in our workplaces that shape our expressions of faith. The author of 1 Peter writes wisely about being God's people in a world that doesn't always welcome this. The entire book is worthy of review; however, 1 Peter 2:16, 17 sum it up: "Exercise your freedom by serving God, not by breaking the rules. Treat everyone you meet with dignity. Love your spiritual family. Revere God. Respect the government."[4] There are no rules against love, respect, reverence, and care for all people. There are no rules in the universe that can separate us from constant inner communion with our Lord.

We live, however, in a pluralistic society. Rules govern outward expressions of our faith. At this point in history, a public school teacher does not have the liberty to lead class in oral prayer. We have no right to withhold civil liberties from those who differ with our beliefs. We're governed by hiring regulations. The law is trying to do what we should be doing all along—loving everyone all of the time. When that's the spirit of the law, we have no quarrel with it. We gladly abide by both spirit and the letter of such rules.

On the other hand, sometimes rules violate conscience. For example, some can't participate in the military due to conviction that it violates the highest law—love. There are jobs we can't accept, contracts we can't bid on, grants we can't seek, conditions of federal funding we can't endorse. We abide by the laws of our nation, the rules of our communities, and the policies of our organizations unless they violate the kingdom of God. Then we have no choice but to follow the higher law. We do so in humility, in love and respect for those with whom we differ. We accept consequences of noncompliance. We count it a blessing to participate in the suffering of Jesus.

Witness to People Who Are Wrong

In every workplace there are people who are wrong. Their ideas may be mistaken, their lifestyles repugnant, their values bankrupt. Jesus models how we should be with people we consider wrong. The Luke 19 Zacchaeus narrative offers insight. Here was a man who was wrong. He was an extortionist.[5] If there was anyone in the crowd Jesus should have upbraided, it was Zacchaeus. But watch what Jesus did. He singled him out. He spotted the little man in the tree, stopped his entourage, and honored him by doing the unthinkable—coming to dinner.[6]

We don't know what the evening's conversation held. But we certainly have no record of Jesus condemning this very wrong man. In fact, we're led to believe Jesus didn't preach a sermon. We do see that being noticed and valued by Jesus causes Zacchaeus to set his business in order—at quite a cost. We can imagine Zacchaeus was not going to be quite as rich after he followed the Jewish formula for restitution!

Following Jesus' model, the first step we take is to get to know the person we know or suspect is wrong. People are wrong for interesting and varied reasons. It *is* hard to invite *that* person at work to join you at lunch! These are the last people we want to get to know. But they're *exactly* the ones to whom we're to reach out.

Our outreach has to come from humility. We may be right that the other person's wrong. We also may not have matters completely straight. Only God knows the heart and intentions.[7] We need to walk gently even when sure Scripture is on our side. Pharisees were good Scripture scholars but often didn't have it right. We can boldly speak and live our understanding of Scripture, but this doesn't excuse us from humility, respect, and love for those with whom we differ.

In caring for those we disagree with, we often gain a voice. We have new permissions to say the tough as well as easy things. People can tell when we are really on their side, when we want the best for them. They can accept hard sayings when they know they are loved. It's hard to hear *anything* from people who judge and condemn us. Until we want the best for a person, we haven't earned the right to express our convictions. God is for every human—hook, line, and sinker. We can do no less.

DISCUSSION QUESTIONS

1. What subtle workplace pressures tempt you not to be real about your faith?

2. What rules and regulations prohibit you from certain expressions of faith? Are these rules in the spirit of care and respect? Rules to stand against? How do we oppose in humility and respect?

3. What are the common openings we have in the workplace authentically to share the good news of our life? Have we been overlooking any opportunities?

4. How have people been helpful to us when we've been wrong?

Afterword

God's people have always experienced gaps between what they hoped and believed—and what they could live into. This is not the mark of a bad person, a hypocrite, a failure. It's a mark of a growing person. The answer isn't either to ignore the discrepancy or try harder. The answer is to seek refreshment from the Holy Spirit.

Pentecost was the continental divide of empowerment and courage for the disciples. We come from a variety of traditions regarding the work of the Spirit, but every tradition understands that the Spirit is the gift of God's presence that enables us to live the Good News. And it's to the Holy Spirit that we turn when our lives fall short of our beliefs. There is no condemnation—only comfort, encouragement, invitation, and guidance.

> *Holy Spirit, we invite you into the nooks and crannies of our beings.*
>
> We want to be your people. We want to live immersed in your nature.
>
> Wash over us in cleansing, comfort, and courage.
>
> Our hearts turn joyfully to you as a flower lifts its face to the sun.
>
> May our work be a gift of Love to God and to the earth. Thank you.
>
> *Amen*

Notes

Chapter 1

1. John 15:1-11.
2. Genesis 1, 2; Matthew 14:13-21; Luke 22:47-51.
3. 1 Kings 17:8-10.
4. 2 Kings 4:1-7.
5. Deuteronomy 29:5.
6. John 6:1-14; Matthew 14:13-21; Mark 6:32-44; Luke 9:10-17.
7. Corrie Ten Boom, *The Hiding Place* (New York: Bantam Books, 1971).
8. Leviticus 25:2-24.
9. Joshua 10:12-14.
10. John 3:16; 1 Peter 3:18-20, 4:6.

Chapter 2

1. Daniel 1–4.
2. Genesis 3.
3. George Fox, *The Journal of George Fox* (Richmond: Friends United Press, 1976), 97.
4. Matthew 5–7, special attention to 6:10.
5. Matthew 6:33.
6. John 17; 18:36.
7. John Fischer, *What On Earth Are We Doing: Finding Our Place as Christians in the World* (Ann Arbor: Servant Publications, 1996), 9.
8. 1 Peter 3:18-20; 4:6.

9. John 3:16, 17.

10. Romans 8:28.

11. Leviticus 25; Deuteronomy 5:12-15. For a good discussion of Sabbath principles, I recommend Marva J. Dawn, *Keeping the Sabbath Wholly: Ceasing, Resting, Embracing, Feasting* (Grand Rapids: William B. Eerdmans Publishing Company, 1989).

12. Matthew 5:43-48.

13. Romans 12:2-8.

14. In Aztec religion human sacrifice was believed necessary to keep the planetary system working properly. One ritual was to offer a pre-dawn human sacrifice each day to ensure sunrise.

15. Brother Lawrence. *The Practice of the Presence of God* (Old Tappan, N.J.: Fleming H. Revell Company, 1978), 7-10.

16. R. G. LeTourneau, *Mover of Men and Mountains* (Chicago: Moody Press, 1967).

17. Deuteronomy 7:9.

18. Thomas R. Kelly, *A Testament of Devotion* (San Francisco: Harper Collins, reprint 1996), 65-85.

19. Donald B. Kraybill, *The Upside-Down Kingdom* (Scottdale: Herald Press, 1978), 308-309; see also Kraybill's second edition (Herald Press, 1990), for a fully updated treatment of upside-down kingdom values.

20. Matthew 6:19-20.

Chapter 3

1. I'm using the phrases kingdom of God, monarchy of God, culture of God, realm of God, and society of God interchangeably. While some find kingdom language objectionable, there is no one alternative phrase that truly captures this idea. Instead of eliminating kingdom language, I use several phrases to reflect the many facets of the Covenant gospel order.

2. The Gospel of Matthew uses kingdom of heaven language while the rest of the New Testament writers use kingdom of God language. They mean precisely the same thing. The use of kingdom of heaven in Matthew does not indicate that the kingdom is in future time. Rather it reflects that Matthew is written by a Jewish author to a Jewish audience. Judaism considered the name

of God too holy to be spoken. It was customary to use other phrases as substitutes in conversation. One substitute would have been "heavens of heavens." The author of Matthew is implementing this device in speaking of the kingdom of the heavens of heavens—in short, the kingdom of heaven.

3. Jan Wood, "The Kingdom is Now," *Fruit of the Vine*, April-June 1979, p. 91.

4. Matthew 13:44-45.

5. While the garden hose imagery is helpful for me, I don't want to leave the impression that we're empty conduits in this process. Actually, God joins each of us in a unique relationship or union. Who-we-are joins with who-God-is to bring something special and irreplaceable to each situation. I don't have imagery that fully captures that amazing truth.

6. Brother Lawrence, 8.

7. Ibid., 23.

8. Ibid., 24.

9. Ibid., 8.

10. Matthew 25:21; Luke 16:10; Luke 19:17.

11. Many Scriptures bear witness to this truth, but two may suffice: 1 John 4:7-12 and Matthew 7:21-23.

12. Arthur Raistrick, *Quakers in Science and Industry* (New York: Augustus M. Kelley, Publishers, 1968), 42.

13. Mark 2:27-28.

14. Leviticus 25. The academic community is one sector of the work world that has secularized the practice of sabbatical years. This has been a useful way to prolong the productivity and professional growth of professors. It provides a hedge against burnout. The concept is also useful in the business community. Intel is an example of a company with a sabbatical program.

15. Leviticus 23 and Deuteronomy 16.

16. John 2:1-12.

17. Matthew 15:21-28.

Chapter 4

1. Matthew 7:24. We're used to thinking of mammon as a word for wealth or riches. Those of us who, in the context of an

affluent culture, feel not-rich tend to dismiss this admonition because it seems not really to apply to us. The word more broadly can refer to property and profit. I doubt it would be stretching Jesus' intent to think of mammon as the economic system that indeed becomes a false god generation after generation. The economic system is overwhelmingly influential in our lives. It sets the goals, defines the processes, requires its sacrifices, pays its rewards. The majority of people serve it as if it were the only option. Its message tends to be not parallel to the kingdom's but the opposite. We can't give our lives to both God and the economic system.

2. Matthew 18:1-6.

3. Matthew 8:5-13.

4. Matthew 6:7–34.

5. Ecclesiastes 3:1-15; 3:11.

6. It seems trite to annotate this point with one text. The entire Scripture is about a covenant, a marriage between God and God's people. It's the theme of the biblical narrative. Life in relationship with God is all it was meant to be. Life out of relationship with God is garbage. Garbage is stuff with no value, organization, or meaning. The stuff of life can be lived but has no purpose except to be carted away to the trash. A snapshot of the glory of life lived as marriage is found in Revelation 21:1-7 and 22:17. Psalm 91:14-16 is another tender insight into the intimacy of the divine-human relationship.

7. T. Canby Jones, *George Fox's Attitude Toward War* (Richmond: Friends United Press, 1984). The peace churches have understood that in using spiritual weapons of love, peace, truth, and long-suffering, we follow the example of the Lamb of God, Jesus. This is our model for fighting evil. This is the battle to which God's people are called. It's not a question of whether or not to fight but of what weapons we'll use. Ones that work? Or ones that only add to pain and destruction? One term that arose to describe this upside-down battle is the Lamb's War.

8. Psalm 37 is a wonderful expression of this truth in the Old Testament. Romans 8 is one of the touchstone passages in the New Testament. John 17:20-26 reflects the unity of purpose, methods, and rewards of those who have joined the Lamb.

9. John 9:3; 2 Corinthians 12:8-10; 13: 4.

10. Psalm 56:8-11.

11. Exodus 20:3.

12. Matthew 6:24a.

13. Frank Laubach wrote several books and pamphlets. *Letters by a Modern Mystic* and *Prayer: The Mightiest Force in the World* are two of my favorites. Thomas Kelly's essays have been collected into two classic books, A *Testament of Devotion* and *The Eternal Promise.*

14. Frank Laubach, *Prayer: the Mightiest Force in the World* (New York: Fleming H. Revell Company, 1946), 76. Our stereotype of those who live like this is that they would be "so heavenly minded they were no earthly use." But Laubach is a good example of a hard-headed realist who knew the power of God. He is better known as creator and founder of the Laubach literacy program.

15. Ibid., 75.

16. Matthew 25:29.

Chapter 5

1. Proverbs 9:10.

2. 1 John 4:18.

3. Romans 8:17.

4. Romans 8:31-39.

5. Colossians 1:9-20.

6. Matthew 6:25-34; Luke 12:22-31.

7. Raistrick.

8. Genesis 16.

Chapter 7

1. Matthew 5:11-12.

2. John Finch, *In Love* (Seattle: Southgate Printing, 1985), #133.

Chapter 8

1. Ephesians 6:10-13.

2. Walter Wink, *Naming the Powers: The Language of Power in the New Testament* (Philadelphia: Fortress Press, 1984); *Unmasking the Powers: The Invisible Forces That Determine Human Existence* (Philadelphia: Fortress Press, 1986); *Engaging the Powers: Discernment and Resistance in a World of Domination* (Minneapolis: Fortress Press, 1992).

3. *Unmasking the Powers,* 4.

4. Colossians 1:15-20.

5. Psalm 56:8-11.

6. James 5:12b.

7. Matthew 5:13-16.

Chapter 9

1. Genesis 50:20.

2. Hebrews 13:15.

3. 1 Thessalonians 5:16-18; Merlin R. Carothers, *Prison to Praise: Spiritual Power through Praise* (Plainfield, N.J.: Logos International, 1971).

4. Walter Wink says it another way: "What exposes and confounds them [the Powers], what drives them into a frenzy of rage that blinds them to the elephant trap of God's historical ironies, is being called upon to praise God. . . . Praise is the homeostatic principle of the universe. It preserves the harmony of the whole by preventing usurpation of the whole by its parts. Praise is the ecological principle of divinity whereby every creature is subordinated to its organic relationship with the Creator. *Praise is the cure for the apostasy of the Powers*" (*Engaging the Powers*, 167).

5. One of my favorite books is a devotional classic, *God Calling*, edited by A. J. Russell. This little volume consistently reminds us of the power of gratefulness and daily invites us to remain centered in a thanksgiving spirit.

6. It's fascinating that the human emotions have this inverted. We're convinced we need to be the ones judging and are angry when it's suggested God is the judge. We don't want God to punish because we think God will make mistakes and someone will be separated from God or reap consequences they don't

deserve. Yet we're willing to judge harshly in full knowledge that we make many mistakes. How many innocent persons have we executed? Or how many times has someone of charm or wealth or connections eluded justice? How many times have we been mistaken about what a person was saying or doing? How many misunderstandings and misperceptions have led to incorrect judgments of another? God, who sees the inner workings of our hearts, knows every extenuating circumstance of our being, and sees all, does not err. Who is to be trusted with judgment?

7. Matthew 18:15-35. The first part of this teaching is delineating the steps to take when someone has sinned against us. Our usual reading of verses 15-17 is that we try to reconcile through a series of incremental steps. Then when all fails, we punish by shunning or breaking fellowship. I've often read this passage with the assumption that this is what we do to bring the offender to admit wrong and set it right. I'm wondering if Jesus is telling us when we can be released from concern. I'm suggesting that this entire passage makes more sense if we think about releasing.

Jesus had already been modeling fellowship with Gentiles and tax collectors. So it's doubtful Jesus was recommending punitive silent treatment or isolation. It can't be a "three strikes and you're out" strategy, for he tells Peter to forgive an infinite amount of times. Rather, Jesus is saying, "release them. You've done your part as a faithful member of the community of faith. You can let it go now. God has seen and been present to the process. It's now God's turn to follow through."

Releasing people means not being responsible for their behavior. We don't have to pretend nothing has happened. We're free to be and do whatever love is inclined to do. We don't owe them anything. They don't owe us anything. They're now standing before their God in this matter.

8. 1 Thessalonians 5:17.

9. Richard Foster, *Prayer* (San Francisco: HarperSanFrancisco, 1992). This is one of my favorite books on prayer, although many fine volumes are available.

10. There is an excellent discussion of blessings in Gary Smalley and John Trent's book, *The Blessing* (Nashville: Thomas Nelson Publishers, 1986).

11. John 15.

12. Matthew 20:25-28.

Chapter 10

1. Acts 2.

2. Acts 6, 7.

3. Acts 17:16-34.

4. Eugene H. Peterson, *The Message* (Colorado Springs: NavPress, 1994).

5. The Roman system of tax collection provided a fertile occupation for extortion. The Roman government set the quota for what must be collected by the tax collector. However, individual collectors were free to extract as much as they could from citizens. This was a profitable business. Tax collectors were deeply hated by the Jews. They represented the worst of the Roman tyranny. A parallel in our society might be the Mafia; they were clearly the bad guys.

6. Hospitality in biblical times meant more than sharing something to eat. It was an act of mutual commitment. Those who shared hospitality were making a commitment to do no harm to one another.

7. Hebrews 4:11-13.

Related Resources

Spirituality

Fenelon. *Let Go*. Springdale: Whitaker House, 1973.

Foster, Richard. *Prayer*. San Francisco: HarperSanFrancisco, 1992.

Kelly, Thomas R. A *Testament of Devotion*. San Francisco: HarperSanFrancisco, reprint 1996.

————. *The Eternal Promise*. Richmond: Friends United Press, 1977.

Kelsey, Morton T. *Caring: How Can We Love One Another?* New York: Paulist Press, 1981.

Laubach, Frank. *Prayer, the Mightiest Force in the World*. New York: Fleming H. Revell Company, 1946.

————. *Letters By A Modern Mystic*. Syracuse: New Readers Press, 1955.

Brother Lawrence. *The Practice of the Presence of God*. Old Tappan: Fleming H. Revell Company, 1978.

Russell, A. J., ed. *God Calling*. Old Tappan, N.J.: Fleming H. Revell Company, 1980.

Steere, Douglas V. *Prayer and Worship*. Richmond: Friends United Press, 1978.

Woolman, John. *The Journal of John Woolman*. Secaucus, N.J.: The Citadel Press, 1972.

Spiritual Aspects of the Life of Work

Dawn, Marva J. *Keeping the Sabbath Wholly: Ceasing, Resting, Embracing, Feasting.* Grand Rapids: William B. Eerdmans Publishing Company, 1989.

Ellul, Jacques. *Money and Power.* Downers Grove, Ill.: Inter-Varsity Press, 1984.

Fischer, John. *What On Earth Are We Doing? Finding Our Place as Christians in the World.* Ann Arbor, Mich.: Servant Publications, 1996.

Foster, Richard. *The Freedom of Simplicity.* San Francisco: Harper & Row Publishers, 1981.

———. *Money, Sex and Power: The Challenge of the Disciplined Life.* San Francisco: HarperSanFrancisco, 1985.

Griffin, Emilie. *The Reflective Executive: A Spirituality of Business and Enterprise.* New York: Crossroad, 1993.

Kraybill, Donald B. *The Upside-Down Kingdom.* Scottdale: Herald Press, 1978; rev. ed., 1990.

MacDonald, Gordon. *Ordering Your Private World.* New York: Oliver Nelson, 1984.

Palmer, Parker. *The Active Life: A Spirituality of Work, Creativity and Caring.* San Francisco: Harper & Row, 1990.

Stringfellow, William. *An Ethic for Christians and Other Aliens in a Strange Land.* Waco, Tex.: Word Books, 1976.

Wallis, Jim. *Agenda for Biblical People: A New Focus for Developing a Lifestyle of Discipleship.* San Francisco: Harper & Row, Publishers, 1976.

Wink, Walter. *Naming the Powers: The Language of Power in the New Testament.* Philadelphia: Fortress Press, 1984.

————. *Unmasking the Powers: The Invisible Forces That Determine Human Existence.* Philadelphia: Fortress Press, 1986.

————. *Engaging the Powers: Discernment and Resistance in a World of Domination.* Minneapolis: Fortress Press, 1992.

The Author

Jan Wood is a recorded Friends minister and graduate of the University of California at Berkeley and of Seattle Pacific University. She brings a diversity of work experience to her writing. She has pastored local congregations in Washington and Indiana and has served as a campus minister. She was Chair of Religion and Philosophy at Wilmington College of Ohio and later Associate Vice-President for Academic Affairs. She is presently Director of Good News Associates, Seattle, Washington.

The mother of three daughters, Jan is active in the Religious Society of Friends (Quakers) and attends Friends Memorial Church, Seattle. She is a popular speaker and retreat leader.

Beth Oppenlander, a graduate of Seattle Pacific University, is working toward a master's degree in business administration. The focus of her studies is the integration of theology and business management. Her insights and observations made important collaborative contributions to this book. She and her husband live in Seattle and attend Shoreline Covenant Church.

About Herald Press, Pandora Press, and Pandora Press U.S.

Responding to challenges and opportunities of a changing publishing world amid shared visions, three presses have developed innovative relationships. Herald Press can efficiently produce and distribute books selling in the thousands. Pandora Press and Pandora Press U.S. are pioneering ways economically to publish shorter runs.

By coordinating their programs, the presses can match their respective strengths with what best suits a given book, share in Herald's ability to provide marketing support, and experience rewarding synergies as the Pandoras enable Herald to support publication of an even wider variety of books that fit the Herald Press mission.

The story begins with **Herald Press**, Scottdale, Pennsylvania. Largest of the presses and long a Mennonite denominational publisher, Herald publishes Anabaptist-Mennonite books that address honestly and creatively such issues as peace and social concerns, a biblical understanding of Christian faith, the mission of the church, and the importance of marriage and family. Herald Press aims to offer church and world the best in thinking and spiritual leadership.

Herald Press

Pandora Press, Kitchener, Ontario, was founded in 1995 to make available, at reasonable cost to publisher and public, short runs of books dealing with Anabaptist, Mennonite, and Believers Church topics, both historical and theological. Pandora Kitchener provided models and inspiration for Pandora U.S.

Pandora Press U.S., Telford, Pennsylvania, was founded in 1997 by a former Herald editor after Herald, though still committed to scholarly books, elected to release fewer. Seeking gospel light in a Pandora's box of questions, complexities, opportunities, Pandora U.S. publishes thought-provoking theological, scholarly, and popular books of interest to Anabaptist, Mennonite, Christian, and general readers.

Though fully independent, the two Pandoras support each other by consulting on books each publishes, contracting for each other's services, and coordinating distribution and marketing to develop distinct but related images for their similarly named ventures.

Christians at Work, produced through prepress by Pandora U.S., then printed, marketed, and distributed by Herald Press with Pandora U.S. imprint, exemplifies coordinated publishing.